Mirror of Love

Mirror of Love

*Meditations on the
Sufi Path of Love*

BOOK I:
INSPIRATIONS

Pir Netanel Miles-Yépez

The Inayati-Maimuni Order
Boulder, Colorado
2023

*"The old shall be renewed,
and the new shall be made holy."*
— Rabbi Avraham Yitzhak Kook

Albion-Andalus, Inc.
P. O. Box 19852
Boulder, CO 80308
www.albionandalus.com

Design and composition by Albion-Andalus Books
Cover design by Samantha Krezinski
Cover image of "The mystic Aḥmad Ghazzalī, talking to a disciple." Persian miniature from the manuscript *Majalis al-Ushshaq* ('Meetings of the lovers'), 1552, within a Silver Gilt Leaf Persian Constellation Mirror and designs by Daniel Jami'.

ISBN: 978-1-953220-17-2 (Hardcover)
ISBN: 978-1-953220-36-3 (Paperback)

Manufactured in the United States of America

For the Friend-Beloved

"Whatever name I may mention,
It is to her I am alluding;
Whatever the house I may sing in elegy,
It is her house of which I am thinking."

— Muhyī ad-Dīn ibn ʿArabī

Contents

Mirror of Love

Part IV: *Love is an Affliction*

Meditations on the Sufi Path of Love

Part V: *The Drama of Love*

Part VI: *The Separation of Lover & Beloved*

Mirror of Love

Part VII: *The Courts of Love*

Preface

This book has its origins in a far older book, the classic Sufi treatise on love by Aḥmad Ghazzalī, called the *Sovāneh*, which helped me through the most difficult period of my life.

I first opened its pages while teaching at a week-long Sufi retreat in New Lebanon, New York, in the summer of 2015. It was a period of intense heartbreak and loss for me, and I brought the book along (in Nasrollah Pourjavady's translation), hoping to find some understanding in it for all that had happened in my life (or perhaps, like the friend of Ghazzalī who requested he write the *Sovāneh*, merely to console myself by reading about that which I had so recently lost).*

In the brief hours between teaching sessions, I read the first four or so chapters in a narrow room built by the celibate Shakers more than a hundred years earlier. Though littered with tangled metaphors and obscure references, I was fascinated by the book, and recognized something of my own journey in its mystical evocations of love. Indeed, the passionate energies and dynamics of attraction it described seemed to come to life all around me in the steamy air of summer in the Berkshires, intensifying my experience of its words.

A week later, I left the Berkshires and returned to my home in Colorado where I began to ponder the book's mysteries one honeyed drop at a time. Sometimes I read no more than a single difficult paragraph or page in an entire

---

* Aḥmad Ghazzalī. *Sawānih: Inspirations from the World of Pure Spirits.* Tr. Nasrollah Pourjavady. Lahore, Pakistan: Suhail Academy, 1986: 16.

Mirror of Love

day or week, or just as little in a month. And yet, I carried the book with me everywhere, whether reading it or not, like a lover's talisman. It traveled with me on walks to the lake near my home, to cafés, to doctor's appointments and dinner parties. I took it on spiritual pilgrimages to Devils Tower in Wyoming and Black Elk Peak in South Dakota. It even accompanied me as I fell in love again, traveling the country for the next two years on a magical journey of awakening. Thus, I read this obscure medieval treatise amid unexpectedly romantic vistas—on blankets on hillsides in Asheville, North Carolina and Memphis, Tennessee, at Sufi 'traveler's houses' in San Francisco and Washington D.C., and in absolute contentment on cool beaches in the gentle coves of Cape Ann in northeastern Massachusetts.

For nearly three years, I read and traveled with the *Sovāneh*—my companion through the twists and turns of love—until finally, on an Easter morning, in a little hotel room in Virginia, almost as small as the Shaker cell in which I had first opened the book, I read its final chapters in much the same state as I had begun it, alone and heartbroken, desperate for it to tell me something that might help me to understand the significance of my own painful journey with love.

Truth be told, I didn't always like what it had to say, anymore than I always understood or agreed with it. Sometimes I read it grudgingly and defiantly, almost against my will. Indeed, as I read its final chapters amid tears and feelings of anguish, I somehow felt that I should have learned or internalized something from it by then that could have alleviated all the pain I was then experiencing. But the *Sovāneh* is not a cure; it is the tale of a sickness, the story of how the disease of love works on its victim, progressing through three difficult stages of dying into love. Thus, in the end, I found myself just another patient reading about the inevitable progress of his own terminal illness.

Nevertheless, those three years were a laboratory of love for me, in which I experienced nearly all of love's most profound joys and painful lessons. In the space of that time, my marriage of more than two decades ended; I fell in love with and quickly lost a woman for whom I had given up everything, leaving me suicidal; and I discovered the most rich and challenging experience of love I had ever known, only to lose that, too, as if by the *Sovāneh*'s own design. Love had become my most severe teacher and the *Sovāneh* my guide.

After finishing the *Sovāneh* and returning home, I rose from my bed one morning with a sudden clarity and began to write the first pages of two new books: one, a distillation of the Sufi 'path of love,' according to my own understanding of it; and the other, the book you are now reading. Having finally completed my own slow reading of the *Sovāneh*—and having witnessed myself in nearly every state of love—I now read it again (this time, quickly) as a prelude to my own writing process.

For even as I read the *Sovāneh*'s first chapters years before, I felt an immediate desire to make its ideas more intelligible to a contemporary audience, to write about Sufism and its understanding of love (as a transformative spiritual path) in a way that was more relevant to modern spiritual seekers, and not merely to those like myself with the patience and learning to enter into the obscure mysteries of Ghazzalī, 'Ayn al-Quzāt, 'Erāqī, or Suhrawardī. Indeed, I wanted to update these same teachings and apply them to the most relevant spiritual practice of our day… *relationship.*

Mirror of Love

But, before I could make these ideas truly accessible, I first needed to deal with them in their raw form, as they are contained in the *Sovāneḥ*.

The *Sovāneḥ (Sawāniḥ* in Arabic, meaning, 'inspirations') was written in Farsi (Persian) around the year 1114, and is comprised of seventy-seven short chapters and a prologue, composed by Aḥmad Ghazzalī (ca. 1061–1123)—founder of the Sufi 'school of love,' and brother of the famous Sufi theologian, Abū Ḥāmid Muḥammad Ghazzalī (ca. 1058-1111)—at the request of his friend, Sā'in ad-Dīn, who wished to have an account of Ghazzalī's extemporaneous thoughts on the subject of love. And the book is just that, an unsystematic—though highly sophisticated—series of reflections on the metaphysical dynamics of love.[*]

The *Sovāneḥ* was innovative in its time, not only because it articulated a vision of romantic love as a path to God (a vision that would come to influence the Christian West through the Troubadours and the Arthurian romances), but also because it incorporated both poetry and stories into a body of descriptive prose (a fact which makes perfect sense when one remembers that the book was not a formal treatise, but a series of written reflections addressed to a friend). Thus, the author often turns aside to tell an illustrative story, or even, according to the conversational norms of Persian culture, to recite some lines of poetry.

But the *Sovāneḥ is* difficult, precisely because it *is* unstructured and unsystematic, and more so because its ideas are complex, pointing to a mystical reality and system of values that is not obvious to the reader. It is also difficult for the modern reader of English because it is essentially a medieval work, written in the 12th-century by a Persian

---

[*] See Pourjavady's introduction in Ghazzalī, *Sawāniḥ*, 4-6.

xiv

Meditations on the Sufi Path of Love

Muslim writing in his native tongue, while also using a coded language familiar to Sufis alone (and not even to all of them). Thus, the unsuspecting and uninitiated reader of Nasrollah Pourjavady's scholarly English translation from the Farsi—*Sawānih: Inspirations from the World of Pure Spirits*— might find themselves struggling to navigate an English style which mirrors the inspirational immediacy and highly idiosyncratic medieval prose and poetry of a Persian genius.

In rendering the *Sovāneh*'s teachings myself, I wished to remove these barriers for the reader, and to make them more accessible to modern English-speaking Sufis. *I did not, however, intend to make the teachings any less difficult.*

Today, a great many spiritual books are written for popular consumption, as 'beginner books,' often talking about spiritual subjects in banal and superficial terms, so as to make them marketable to 'self-help' consumers. That is not to disparage introductory works, whose value is undeniable; but there is now a glut of such works. More serious works for those who are already committed to a path are rarer. And rarer still are the works on the most difficult and profound teachings. The *Sovāneh* is of the latter type.

In *Mirror of Love*, I have attempted to preserve the depth of these teachings, and much of their original presentation. However, it is *not* a translation of Aḥmad Ghazzalī's *Sovāneh*. That has already been ably accomplished, as I have noted above. Rather, *Mirror of Love* is a 'reflection' of the *Sovāneh*, or more precisely, a reflection on the specific teachings of its seventy-seven short chapters and prologue. Thus, I have subtitled the book, "Meditations on the Sufi Path of Love."

This is accurate, as my writing process was both simple *and* meditative. I would read a single chapter or passage in Pourjavady's translation, close my eyes a moment, and then,

Mirror of Love

almost without thinking, write the substance of Ghazzalī's teaching as I understood it, in my own words (occasionally going back to check myself against the original). I did this day after day for more than a month (perhaps up to three months) until I had completed the full draft of what you have before you, likely by the summer of 2018.

I then put the book 'in a drawer' for a time while I worked on the initial chapters of the other book I had started, *A Poisoned Cup*, which was to be my own more targeted and accesible distillation of the Sufi 'path of love.' I did not return to *Mirror of Love* again until late 2019, when I began to give talks or commentaries on its chapters for *soḥbet* after our weekly community *zikr*. These talks, given to Inayati-Maimuni murīds, were eventually transcribed and edited for inclusion in two further volumes of commentary.

In January of 2022, I finally decided to finish *Mirror of Love*, polishing each chapter and creating some organization for them; for in the *Sovāneḥ*, Ghazzalī writes his seventy-seven 'inspirations' as they occur to him, pursuing an idea in one chapter and often abandoning it entirely for a completely different idea in the next, with little or no thought given to the book's organization or the development of its ideas. Thus, I have rearranged the *Sovāneḥ*'s seventy-seven teachings according to broad themes—"Following Beauty into Love," "The Drama of Love," "The Separation of Lover and Beloved," *et cetera*—and created a glossary of key words and concepts.

Anticipating the desire of some to read *Mirror of Love* as a kind of meta-commentary on the *Sovāneḥ*, or simply to know how a particular chapter in *Mirror of Love* connects to the *Sovāneḥ*, I have also provided a table of correspondences in the back of the book.

In suggesting such correspondences with the *Sovāneḥ*, I do not mean to assume for my own work any of the latter's well-earned reputation, or, God forbid, to diminish that reputation by associating it with my own deficiences. *Mirror of Love* is, in the end, simply a personal 'inspiration,' born of gratitude to the founding master of the *mazhab-i 'eshq*, the Sufi 'school of love,' for hard lessons learned, and, as an acknowledgement of the enduring power of these teachings, even after more than 900 years.

At an early stage of this journey, when my relationship to the *Sovāneḥ* was still new, an elder Sufi mentor of mine, Murshid Thomas Atum O'Kane, hearing me near despair, wisely advised me to "make a monument to love," as an expression of all that I was then experiencing, perhaps hoping that such an effort might help me survive my own internal tumult. That monument is still unfinished, but this work, such as it is, is the foundation.

Netanel Mu'in ad-Din Miles-Yépez
Boulder, Colorado, March 14ᵗʰ, 2022

"God is Truth,
And Truth is God."
— *The Bowl of Saqi*

Note to the Reader

In this work, the terms 'lover' and 'beloved' are used to denote the seeker and the sought. Because the lover is always at a disadvantage and frequently suffering, this may lead some readers to believe that the dynamics suggested here are indicative of a one-sided, abusive relationship. This, however, would be a mistake. Here we are simply following the *lover's* journey and transformation in love, just as any other spiritual manual might outline the *seeker's* quest for enlightenment and spiritual maturity (in which the master might stand in place of the beloved). Thus, the teaching is less about relationship than it is about the nature of love, and how it works on the lover. In relationship, each is ideally playing both roles, 'lover' and 'beloved,' the power and vulnerability passing back and forth between them.

— N.M-Y.

Mirror of Love

Prologue

Love is not expressed in words or contained in sentences, my friend; its experience defies all description, its purity so ineffable that no sullied or imperfect word may touch it. Thus, we distinguish the love itself *('eshq)* from the mystical ideas *(ma'ānī)* of love, and the expressions of those ideas *('ibārat),* which are really only allusions *(ishārat).* And yet, it is difficult to convey any meaning to one who has not tasted *(zawq)* something themselves. Thus, the allusions to things tasted are made to help, and may even connect one to the inner vision *(basīrat)* required to make and understand such allusions in the first place.

> Thirsting for the wine of her mouth,
> I take to drinking from the bottle.
> But can the bottle really replace
>   what passes those lips?
>
> No, friend; but it may soothe
>   an ailing heart for an hour.
> Every physician has a prescription
>   for what ails you;
> But what lasting cure is there
>   outside of Laylā? *

---

* Laylā, the forbidden love of the poet Majnūn.

Part I
Following
Beauty into Love

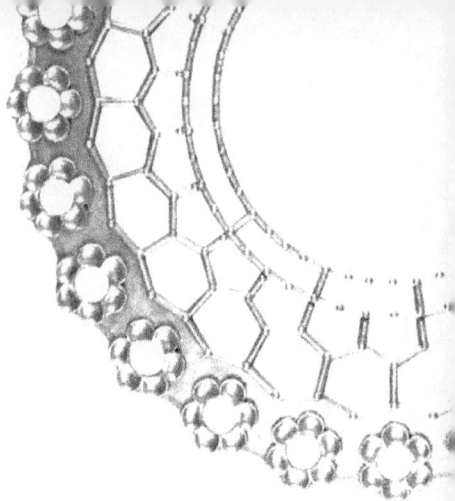

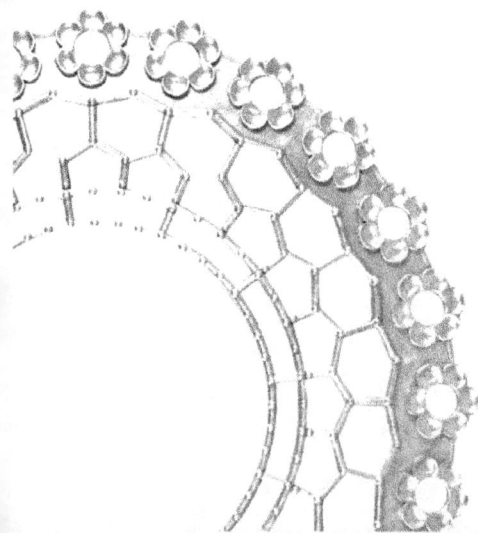

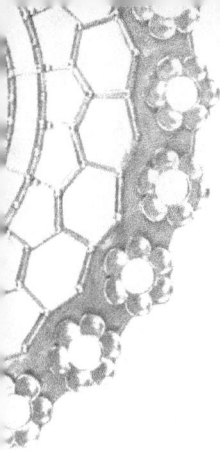

One
The Love of Beauty

"God is beautiful and loves beauty."
— *Ṣaḥīh Muslim*

Either one must be in love with that beauty *(jamāl)*, or with the lover of the beauty. This is a profound secret. Lovers only see, know, and want the object of God's contemplation, the effect of beauty, and the focus of God's love. They care for nothing else. And yet, it may happen that the lover's heart unknowingly seeks the source of that beauty and contemplation, searching diligently until it is found.

Two
The Face of Loveliness

The secret face of everything is divinity. The sign of divinity concealed in creation is loveliness *(ḥusn)*. The secret face is always facing God. Unless one sees that secret face, one will see neither the sign in creation, nor the loveliness. That face is the beauty of God's face reflected in creation, as it says in the holy Qur'ān, "and what remains is the face of your sustainer." (55:27)

7

Three
The Secret of Love

The secret of love is hidden in *'eshq*. The word is comprised of three letters—*'ayin*, *shīn*, and *qāf*. The *'ayin* and *shīn* represent love, *'esh*, and the *qāf*, the heart or *qalb* in which it dwells. When the heart is not in love, it is an organ without a purpose; when it falls in love, it finds itself.

Love begins with the eye *('ayin)* and seeing beauty. This is suggested by the *'ayin* at the beginning of the word *'eshq*. The lover then begins to drink the wine *(sharāb)* of longing *(shawq)*, both suggested by the *shīn* in the middle of the word. When the lover dies to the self and is born again through the beloved, a subsistence *(qīyām)* through love is achieved, which is suggested by the letter *qāf* at the end of the word.

Indeed, there are many secrets to be found in the combinations of these letters, but this is enough for awakening some understanding. Opening the door even a crack is enough for the intelligent seeker.

Four
The Function of the Heart

All of our organs have a function: the function of the eyes is to see, the function of the ears to hear. In the same way, the function of the heart is to love. If the eyes do not see, the ears do not hear, or the heart does not love, then they are not fulfilling their function and are useless.

The heart was created for love and knows nothing else. When it becomes a lover, then its function is fulfilled.

The tears that the heart sends to the eyes are born of the heart's love and compassion. Because love begins with sight, the pain of the heart is connected with the eyes. Thus, the heart sends its messengers to the eyes, as a reminder of its pain, and to urge them to send back another report of the beloved.

Five
The Seed of Beauty
& The Beginnings of Love

When the seed of beauty *(jamāl)* is sown in the cultivated earth of the heart's solitude by the hand of witness *(mushāhadah)*, love begins to grow. This love is then nurtured under the sun of attention *(nazar)*. This is the way of love in general; but occasionally, love also appears to flower spontaneously, co-arising with the awareness of beauty, or even with the awareness of beauty following after love. And yet, in truth, the process always begins with the witness of beauty; for sometimes the witness proceeds from seeing the external form, and sometimes from an internal vision *(basīrat)*.

> The love of all lovers begins with seeing;
> The eye is witness and the affair begins.
> Many a bird enters the cage desiring the seed,
> Many a moth enters the flame desiring its light.

Mirror of Love

In reality, love is the conjunction of two hearts, two mirrors placed before one another, the love reflected in both. And yet, the love of the lover, and that of the beloved, are two different things: the love of the lover for the beloved is the true love; while the love of the beloved is a reflected love, being the love of the lover reflected in the mirror of the beloved.

Since there is a conjunction of hearts, a relational dynamic exists between lover and beloved in which the lover is in a position of helplessness, suffering, and submission, while the beloved is in a position of tyranny, oppression, and pride.

> Standing in the glory of her
>   heart-rending beauty,
> I find that I am not good enough for her;
> And yet she suits me well!

Which is the lover, and which the beloved, is a great mystery. The attraction and pull of loveliness and love are like two entwined and undulating snakes, among whom a mouth may open on either end at any given moment.

From the divine perspective, the beloved's attraction for the lover comes first, calling the lover into existence to accomplish love, as it says in the holy Qur'ān, "God loves them, and they love God." (5:54) For this reason, Bāyazīd Bistāmī said, "For a long time, I was deluded in thinking that I loved God; but later, I found that it was God who had loved me first."

Six
The Mirror of the Lover's Love

The eye of loveliness *(ḥusn)* is shut to its own beauty *(jamāl)*, unable to perceive its perfect loveliness except in the mirror of the lover's love. Thus, beauty needs a lover, so that the beloved can take sustenance from its own beauty in the mirror of the lover's love and quest *(talab)*. This is a great secret and the key to many others.

> My intoxication with her
>   is not without reason—
> There was a tavern, there was wine,
>   and no shortage of delight.
> But do not say it was I alone
>   who sought her;
> For beauty, too, sought a mirror.

In this way, the lover knows the beloved's loveliness better than the beloved, for it is only through the lover that the beloved is nourished by their own loveliness and beauty. This is why the lover feels so possessive. Though captive to the beloved's beauty, the lover actually knows it more intimately than the beloved, and thus has a feeling of ownership. In this sense, the lover is more the beloved than the lover.

In time, love's connection may grow to the point where the lover believes they are actually the beloved, like those intoxicated friends of God who said, "I am the Truth" and "Glory be to me; how great is my majesty!" *

---

* Mansūr al-Hallāj and Bāyazīd Bistāmī.

11

Mirror of Love

In the state of separation *(firāq)*, the lover can make no sense of it, because they are absorbed with and become the beloved. And yet, to speak of this union while separated is a falsehood.

> There is so much love in me for you
> That I sometimes think you are in love with me.
> So either I'll pitch the tent of delight and union,
> Or lose my head over this delusion.

Seven
Love's Aspiration

There is an aspiration *(himmat)* embedded in love. The lover desires a beloved who has a sublime quality. Thus, the lover does not want to accept just any beloved who may fall into the snare of union. It is this aspiration which is responsible for Iblis' answer to God. For when God said, "My curse shall be upon you" (Qur'ān 38:78), Iblis responded, "I swear by your glory" (38:82). By this Iblis meant that love of the glory of God was paramount; nothing else mattered, and to nothing lesser would the angel give reverence; for if anything else was worthy of reverence, God would not be perfect.

Part II
The Evolution of Love

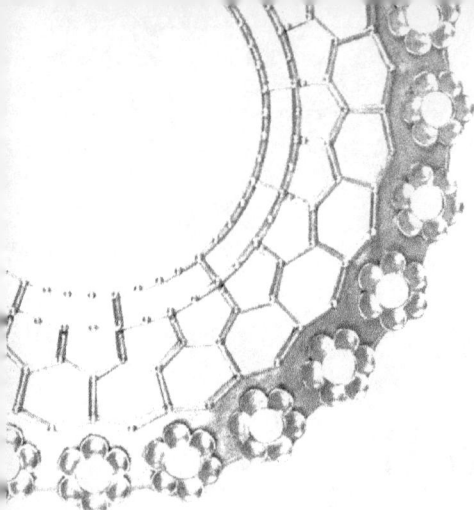

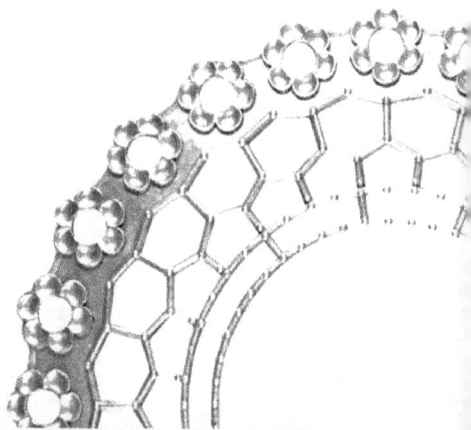

Eight
Clean and Dirty Desire

Desire has two faces, one clean and one dirty: the one focused on the beloved's generosity is clean; the one focused on the lover's merit is dirty.

⚜

Nine
The Lover's Lie

Falling in love, the lover becomes a liar.

From the moment the lover is aware of the possibilities of union with the beloved, the presence of the beloved is established in the lover's imagination. The beloved is then experienced as a *lover* of the lover in the imagination, and the lover of the beloved takes immediate sustenance from the imagination, while knowing it is a lie.

As long as the lover is a lover through the self, and not through the beloved, the lover is a liar, and still afraid of blame and death. But as the lover is increasingly subdued by love, the lies slowly become the truth, and the lover is set free of lies.

In the beginning, the light of love illuminates the interior of the lover, but is hidden from the beloved. This is a lie. The lover may hide this love from the beloved for some time, while continuing to make love to the beloved within.

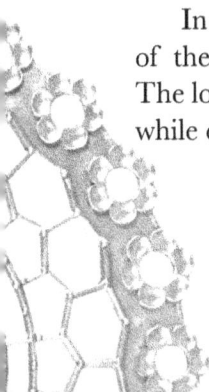

When this defect is removed and the lover surrenders, then the light will illuminate and claim both the inside and the outside; the light will shine upon the lover's face as the totality of the self is given to love. Oneness pervading, how can one cover the face?

⸱⸱⸱ ⸱⸱⸱ ⸱⸱⸱

Ten
Selfish Love

In the beginning, the lover's desire for the beloved is selfish. Without knowing it, the lover is in love with the self through the beloved, and seeks to use the beloved in pursuit of the ego's own desire.

> I said: "You are the idol in the niche of my soul!"
> You replied: "Speak not of the soul then,
>   idolater!"
> I asked: "Why should you cut me with the sword
>   of this argument?"
> You replied: "Because you are still in love
>   with yourself."

When love truly begins to shine in its perfection, illuminating the lover within, the lover then begins to act for the beloved's sake, yielding life itself to please and serve the beloved's need. This is love; everything else is foolishness and delirium.

Eleven
The Faces of Blame,
The Swords of Jealousy,
The Deaths Into Love

Love is perfected in blame *(melāmet)*. With regard to love, there are three faces of blame: one that effaces the world (and receives its censure); one that effaces the self (and makes the sacrifice); and one that effaces the beloved (and loses them in love).

These are accompanied by three swords of jealousy *(ghayrat)* which cut the lover's attachment to anything but love. The sword of the beloved's jealousy guards the lover's attention, cutting it off from everything else. The sword of time's jealousy keeps the lover from devoting any attention to themselves. The sword of love's jealousy forces the lover to take sustenance from love alone, cutting the lover's attachment to the object of love, until there is nothing but love.

> Nothing in the world do I seek from you
>   but love;
> Your union and separation are the same to me.
> Without your love, my being is in chaos,
> So choose what you wish, separation or union.

The sword of love's jealousy is necessary, for the process of love may reach a point at which the beloved is also an obstacle. This is the magnetic power of love's splendor,

Mirror of Love

drawing one to the source of love's sustenance in perfect union *(ittiḥād)*, where there is no room for the separation of lover and beloved, where lover and beloved yield their identities and attachments to love.

The lover who thinks of union *(wiṣāl)* as 'coming together,' taking sustenance from this thought, does not realize the true nature of love.

> If I cried out for your help,
> It would be a betrayal of love,
>   as if I were not in love.
> Impose what 'separation,'
>   demand what 'union' you wish,
> Your love is enough for me!

Love devours both separation and union. With union in love's mouth *(hawsalah)*,* tasted and stored there, what terrors does separation hold?

This is not something everyone can understand: union separates one from the self, thus separation is union, and having is not-having.

Not everyone can find their way to this station *(maqām)* of knowledge, for it begins beyond the boundaries. This reality is a pearl concealed in a shell which lies in the depths of the ocean. However, when knowledge is drowned, the pearl may be found. It will seem as if the pearl has entered the diver's hand; but it is actually the diver that has fallen into the pearl's hand.

---

* The pouch beneath a bird's beak where food is stored.

The Sword of the Beloved's Jealousy (The Death of the World)

If any part of the lover's attention is directed to anything other than the beloved, even if it be as thin as a hair, then the sword of the beloved's jealousy must cut it. The lover must think only of the beloved; the world and its blame mean nothing in comparison.

The lover's reward and refuge are found within. As the prophet said, "I seek refuge in you from you." Both hunger and satisfaction are found there. The lover has nothing to do with the outside world.

> This is the arena of blame,
>   the battlefield of ruin;
> This is the path of gamblers
>   who lose everything;
> This is the brave road of Qalandars
>   in garments torn,
> Who walk with dignity amid destruction,
>   without fear.

The beloved's jealousy demands the destruction of the world. The lover must turn from it without fear.

> Let the world say what it will, my love,
> Blame and name go hand in hand!
> For your sake, my beloved, who cares?
> For love let the world break
>   and bury itself in dust!

Mirror of Love

The Sword of Time's Jealousy
(The Death of the Self)

When the lover has passed the test of denying the world, the beloved's jealousy is roused again. Love and the beloved demand the sacrifice of the self, wielding the sword of time's jealousy, which keeps the lover from devoting time or attention to themselves. The lover is so enamored with the beloved that little time is left for the lover's own concerns; the beloved's concerns are substituted for the lover's.

The Sword of Love's Jealousy
(The Death of the Beloved)

Denying the self, the lover then faces the sword of love's jealousy, forcing the lover to turn from the beloved to love alone; for the lover's self-denial was born of coveting the beloved. Now, all such possessiveness is cut and burned away, and the lover transcends even the beloved for the sake of love. Love's jealousy demands this, forcing the lover to take sustenance from love alone, purifying them of all selfishness, leaving the lover without self or other.

> Beyond the limit of knowledge,
> A gnostic barrier leads to ruin;
> The rough waves of love's ocean
> Break on themselves and return home.

Twelve
The Death of Love

There is also the blame *(melāmet)* the lover feels when perfection is reached in the death of love, when love recedes to an inner chamber. Then, feeling foolish before love's disappearance, the lover is ashamed inside, and before others and the beloved. Thus, pain takes the place of love for a while. The pain will penetrate as far as it can. However, it too will vanish and yield to something new eventually. This is a process that may occur again and again. Love covers its face, veils itself, avoiding amorous contact, and pain makes its appearance, because love is a chameleon, changing color and adapting to every circumstance, in every moment. Sometimes it says, "I have gone away," when in fact it has not.

Thirteen
The Hidden Love

When love attains perfection in the lover, in the absence of the beloved, it hides in the unseen and leaves the external world of the lover's knowledge *('ilm)*. Thus, love appears to be absent, and the lover feels as if it is gone. But it is not gone: the lover is comprehended by love and cannot comprehend it.

Mirror of Love

The sense of love's 'absence' continues for a time; but it is only temporary. The love is journeying inward to seat itself in the innermost chamber of one's being. This is one of the most difficult ideas to understand, though it may be that to which the poet alludes . . .

When affection reaches its perfection,
'Friendship' is transformed into enmity.

Part III
Lover and Beloved

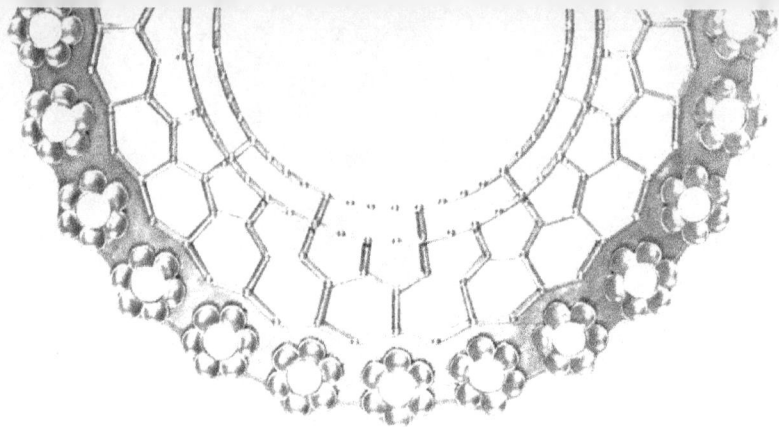

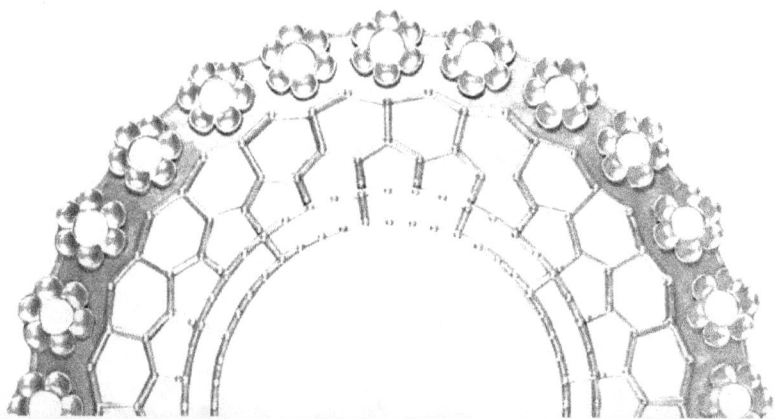

Fourteen
The Origins of Lover and Beloved

The words *'āshiq* and *ma'shūq,* 'lover' and 'beloved,' are derived *(ishtiqāq)* from the word *'eshq,* which refers to 'passionate love.' But in another sense, only the *'āshiq* or 'lover' is truly derived from *'eshq,* for the lover is filled with passionate love and is love's steed. The *ma'shūq,* or 'beloved,' on the other hand, is not actually derived from *'eshq,* but *husn,* 'loveliness.'

❦

Fifteen
A Pair of Opposites

The lover and beloved are a pair of opposites, the qualities of each eliciting the opposite in the other. Thus, they do not come together in union except through the self-sacrifice and annihilation *(fanā)* of the lover.

> That green idol, seeing my yellowed face, says—
> "Expect not to achieve union with me;
> You, so clearly my opposite,
> You, the color of autumn, me of spring!"

Mirror of Love

Sixteen
The Attributes of Lover and Beloved

The attributes of the beloved are might, tyranny, self-sufficiency, and pride. While the attributes of the lover are abasement, poverty, helplessness, and need. Thus, love is sustained by the attributes of the lover. The attributes of the beloved do not manifest unless their opposite manifests in the lover. That is to say, the beloved's self-sufficiency is a response to the lover's needfulness; each of the beloved's attributes is a response to an attribute of the lover.

Seventeen
The Signs of the Beloved

The hair, the cheek, the mole, the stature, the eyebrow, the glance, the smile, and even the rebuke of the beloved, are all signs. Each of these signs relate to a place in the lover from which a specific desire and quest *(talab)* arises.

If the sign of love is in the beloved's eye, the lover's sustenance is derived from the beloved's sight and the world of the imagination *(khayāl)*. Thus, the lover is immune to physical imperfections in the beloved, as the eye is the precious pearl of the heart and spirit.

If the sign is in the eyebrow, then the quest originates in the spirit alone. The scout of awe guides that quest, for the eyebrow is above and beyond the eye.

In the same way, each of the other signs indicated by the facial features and expressions of love signify different spiritual or physical quests, as well as imperfections and faults in them. Love's signs appear on the inner screen of the imagination connected with these quests. In this way, the beloved's features indicate the rank and quality of the lover's love.

Eighteen
Differing Pleasures

Nothing is more pleasurable to the lover than suddenly catching sight of the beloved, the beloved unaware of the lover and the lover's great need. In this need, the lover will pray and beg, supplicate and implore the beloved to respond. If the beloved is slow to respond or late in answering, the reason is often that the beloved is taking sustenance from the lover's need. It is a great pleasure to the beloved, though the lover is unaware of it.

Nineteen
The Possessor Never Possessed

Needlessness is the attribute of the beloved; and need, that of the lover. The lover always needs the beloved, but the beloved is needless, always being the beloved.

Mirror of Love

Every night, I cry blood for your sorrow,
Wracked with agony over your absence.

But you, my idol, are content,
    alone in your niche;
How can you know the pain of one
    who spends a night without you?

You, the ravisher of hearts are excused;
You, never knowing sorrow, are excused.

A thousand nights in tears, blood on my pillow;
You, never having spent a night without you,
    excused.

It is a mistake to believe the lover may ever possess the beloved, that even in union the beloved is actually held in the lover's embrace; for the reality of love adorns the beloved with a necklace of riches never diminished, and not with the ring of bond.

Trying to possess the beloved, the lover will lose everything on the battlefield of love; risking religion and all their worldly goods, name and fortune, they will do anything, leave everything behind, fearless even of losing their life, trampling on their chances of happiness in both this and the next world. But they risk only what is their own; the beloved is never at risk, for the beloved is the possessor, never the possession. The lover is the slave of love and the beloved.

When these ideas are understood, then you may learn the truth: it is only when love manifests in its full majesty, unobscured, that the lover comes into maturity through loss, rising above all imperfections, liberated from the thought of gain or loss.

Twenty
Become the Beloved

The beloved said to the lover, "Become me! For if I become you, then the beloved will be in a state of need, and the lover will be greater. But if you become me, the beloved will grow. Both will be beloved, and the lover will disappear. There will be no more need *(nīyāz);* all will be self-sufficiency *(nāz)*, all richness and no poverty."

Twenty-One
Finding the Self in the Flame

Being a self through one's own self is a sign of immaturity in love, of being unripe. The ripening process begins when one begins to love, pursuing the beloved. When the self no longer belongs to the lover, lost in the beloved, the self is reached again within, through and beyond the beloved. Annihilation *(fanā)* becomes the goal *(qiblah)* of subsistence *(baqā')*, the pilgrim circumambulating the *ka'bah* of holiness, passing the border of permanence into impermanence, like the moth passing the threshold into flame. Knowledge cannot comprehend this except in parable. Perhaps these verses I composed in my youth will shed light . . .

With Jamshīd's cup in my hand,
   disclosing all,
The wheel of heaven descends
   and bows before me.

Mirror of Love

> The *ka'bah* of non-being,
>   the *qiblah* of my own being,
> Even the world's genius
>   is intoxicated with me.

The prophet Ibrāhīm, on seeing the moon, the sun, and the star, said, "This is my sustainer" (Qur'ān 6:76-78). Mansūr al-Hallāj and Bāyazīd Bistāmī said, "I am the Truth" and "Glory be to me!" These are but the chameleon changing states *(talwīn)* and far from our rest *(tamkīn)*.

✦ ❦ ✦

Twenty-Two
The Lover's Absence

Although the beloved is present, witnessing and being witnessed by the lover, the lover is absent. If the beloved's presence *(huzūr)* does not produce the lover's absence *(ghaybat)*, as in the tale of Laylā and Majnūn, then it is an amazement *(dahshat)* which may vanish.

In Baghdad, there was a man from the neighborhood of Nahr al-Mu'allā, who loved a woman across the river Tigris, in the neighborhood of Karakh. Each night, he swam across the Tigris to see her and speak with her. One night, looking at her, he noticed a mole on her face and asked, "Have you always had that mole?"

She answered, "I've had it from birth." Then, looking concerned, she added, "For your own sake, I think you better not cross the river again tonight."

The lover did not heed her warning and entered the river again that night. This time, the cold water shocked his system and he drowned; for he had departed with his self, the self that had seen the mole.

> Unaware of being a lover, or of love,
> Nor of myself, or of the beloved.

—————

Twenty-Three
The Lover in the Ocean

The external lover immersed in the ocean of love does not exist to be aware of the self in love; though the lover bound in time *(waqt)*, as it were, may occasionally break the surface and witness the experience like a spectator. Seeing, they may understand, or they may not. The inner worlds are not easily understood. There are myriad veils and marvels that cannot be explained here.

—————

Twenty-Four
The Headless Lover

The lover's path is consumed with the beloved's *thou (tu'ī)*. As the lover, you do not belong to yourself; you belong to the beloved. Self-determination is for the beloved, not for the lover.

Mirror of Love

A slave to selfish desires,
  there is no end of lust and avarice;
Be a lover that you may be free of both.

Holding two objects,
  the path of unity is divided:
The satisfaction of the beloved,
  or the satisfaction of the lover.

Royalty means nothing in our eyes;
None but the poor lover will gain the prize.

So long as you have a head,
  you are of no interest;
This crown is shaped for the headless hero.

Twenty-Five
Perceiving the Beloved

Love is an intoxication whose perfection prevents the lover from seeing or perceiving the beloved's own perfection. This is because the intoxication of love is experienced by the inner sight *(basīrat)*. The lover's essence is dedicated completely to perceiving the beloved's essence; but on reaching the goal, it cannot perceive or recognize the beloved's attributes or affirm them. And yet, as it is said by Abū Bakr *as-Saddīq*, "The inability to perceive the perceiving is itself a perception."

My idol, a lifetime with you
In days of sorrow and delight,
And, by God, I am still unable
To give an account of your goodness.

─── ✤ ───

Twenty-Six
The Beloved Unknown

Although the lover knows something of love, the beloved is
unknown . . .

Your curl is a chain,
    and I, the unhinged one it binds;
Your love is a fire,
    and I, the moth it consumes;
I am the cup for the wine
    of our covenant;
I am familiar with love,
    but you are a stranger to me.

The poor lover exists in the utmost poverty . . .

I am a beggar
    loitering before your tavern,
Begging wine
    from the cup of charity
        at your door;

Mirror of Love

Though estranged in love,
    wounded to the heart,
Just one sip,
    and I'll care not for wound
    or world.

_____ ✻ _____

Twenty-Seven
Reflections of the Beloved

In the beginning, the lover sees reflections of the beloved in everything similar. Thus, even when Majnūn had not eaten for days, upon capturing a deer, he treated it gently and suddenly set it free. Asked for an explanation, he said, "It reminded me of Laylā, to whom no harm must come."

But at a later stage of love, the lover knows of nothing like the beloved; the beloved is utterly unique, and nothing, no substitute of any kind will satisfy in any degree.

There is no consolation for the true lover. Consolation is an imperfection in love. Ecstasy *(wejd)* must grow. Any diminishment in one's yearning *(ishtīyāq)* after union *(wisāl)* indicates imperfection and impurity. Union must fuel the fire of longing *(shawq)*, increasing it, until nothing else satisfies.

_____ ✻ _____

Twenty-Eight
Dreaming of the Beloved

Seeing the image of the beloved in a dream indicates that the beloved is imprinted on the lover's heart, and the lover has turned their eyes and knowledge to the beloved.

But there is a great secret here. Whatever constitutes the lover is not separable from the love of the beloved. Neither remoteness *(bu'd)* nor nearness *(qurb)* can veil this. This is different from remoteness and nearness in the external world.

In the dream, the lover is seeing the surface of the heart from which the image is transmitted to knowledge, so that the lover has a notion of what is behind the veils.

Twenty-Nine
The Breath of Love
& The Beloved's Guardians

There is a wonderful experience in love, wherein the lover witnesses the beloved in the breath *(nafas)*. Because the heart is the residence of the beloved, the breath becomes the beloved's steed, acquiring their fragrance and color, carrying these *in* and *out* before the lover.

This witnessing causes the lover to turn inward to the heart, the residence of the beloved, so that the lover loses all concern for what is outside. Indeed, when the lover is occupied with the breath of the beloved, the beloved without must actually compete with the beloved within.

This is because the witness of the beloved's breath is less burdensome; taking sustenance with the beloved through the inner door is easier than suffering the beloved's self-sufficiency *(nāz)* without.

Mirror of Love

> Seldom do I pass the door of your house,
> Wary of the guards who might harm me;
> But darling idol, know with a certainty,
>   you occupy the niche of my heart;
> Day and night, whenever I want you,
>   I behold you there.

The guards are not only worldly guardians who would obstruct love; that would be an easy obstacle to overcome. There are also the guardians of love's sultanate—the signs of the beloved's beauty, the glance *(kirishmah)* and self-sufficiency *(nāz)*—for which there is no defense, no way to pass, and from which there is no possibility of flight. Dreading the sultanate of love and its gurads, there is no perfect sustenance from love.

Thirty
The Mirror of the Heart

When love makes the house increasingly vacant and the mirror within clean, a form is established in purity and reflected in the heart. The image *(paykar)* is of the beloved, not oneself. Even if one wishes to see oneself, one sees the beloved.

> So fixed is your image in my eye, in my heart,
> Whatever I perceive now, I think it is you.

This is because the way home, to the self, is through love. Not until love has taken everything in the death of the beloved will one see the self. When the image of the beloved is annihilated, we enter a place in love beyond all knowledge and distinctions.

I am my beloved, and my beloved is me;
I and me the occupant of one body.
When you see me, you see my beloved;
When you see my beloved, you see me.

Oh idol, I thought you were my beloved;
I see now, you are none but my own soul.

I have no way of parting from my love;
If ever I were to turn aside from it,
I would lose my self and my religion.*

Thirty-One
Love is a Mirror

Love is a mirror for both lover and beloved. It allows one to see oneself, the other, and all. If love's jealousy succeeds, the lover cannot see anything other than love. The perfect beauty of the beloved may only be witnessed in the mirror of love. This is also true with regard to all perfections *(nāz)* and imperfections *(niyāz)* on either side.

---

* Lines based on Ibn Fārid's *Tā'iyyah.*

Mirror of Love

Thirty-Two
The Beloved's Need

The gaze of the lover drawn to loveliness *(kirishmah-i ḥusn)* looks not at anything but the beloved and love; but the gaze of the beloved *(kirishmah-i maʿshūqī)*—the beloved's glance and alluring gestures, charm and flirtation—are all sustained by the lover, and have no purpose beyond enticing the lover. In this sense, the apparently needless *(nāz)* beloved is in need *(nīyāz)* of the lover.

In the land of Inja, it was the custom of the sultan to take a daily walk through the streets of the capital, both for his own exercise, and so that his subjects might see him and have confidence in his reign; for subjects who do not see their sultan hardly believe in him. But it was also in this way that one of his subjects, seeing the sultan's beautiful countenance on a daily basis, came to fall in love with him. The unfortunate lover was a commoner, whose job it was to heat the furnaces of the public bathhouse, which the sultan passed each day on his walk. Knowing the sultan's schedule by heart, the man took to seating himself near the gates to the bathhouse at just the right time to catch a glimpse of the sultan each day.

Now, the sultan was often accompanied by his vizier on these walks, and the vizier's job was to know all that went on in the sultanate. So it was that the vizier noticed what the sultan had not—that the *gulkhan-tāb*, the furnace-stoker of the public bathhouse had fallen in love with him.*

---

* The *gulkhan-tāb*, the 'furnace-stoker' was one of the lowest occupations in that society, as it was the furnace-stoker's job to carry dung to the furnace.

One day, as the vizier and the sultan were discussing matters of state, the vizier wished to illustrate the importance of the sultan's subjects and said: "Now, for instance, there is the furnace-stoker of the bathhouse who has fallen in love with you . . ."

"What?!" the sultan interrupted.

"Yes, the furnace-stoker."

"How dare he raise his eyes to me in such a way! Call the guard!"

"Your majesty," said the vizier, "may I suggest that you wait a moment before calling the guard? You are famous for your justice. How will it look if you punish a man for something over which he has no control? He has seen your beauty and been captured by it; what can he do?"

The sultan, considering this, did not reply.

On his walk the next day, the sultan passed the bathhouse as usual. But knowing that he was being watched by the furnace-stoker, there was a subtle change in his air that made him still more beautiful. He now had the air of one who knows they are loved and whose beauty increases with that knowledge.

Just as he was passing out of sight, he turned and glanced at the furnace-stoker, knowing that the latter loved him, and knowing that this look would increase his love.

Thus, the sultan began to pass the bathhouse each day with this subtle change in him, adding the glance of the beloved *(kirishmah-i ma'shūqī)* to the glance that looks on beauty *(kirishmah-i ḥusn)*, until one day the sultan noticed to his dismay that the furnace-stoker was not sitting in his accustomed place as he passed! And as he was not there to witness the sultan's beauty, nor to receive the glance of the beloved, it fell to the ground, useless. There was no one to receive it.

The sultan was upset, saying to the vizier in exasperation: "Where is the furnace-stoker? He is not in his usual place. Why is he neglecting his duties at the bathhouse? Has something happened to him?"

But the clever vizier, seeing that what he wished the sultan to know was now ripe, only said: "Your majesty, do you remember how I said it was useless to punish him for something that was not his fault? Now we can see that his *'need'* was necessary, too."

Thirty-Three
The Beloved Becomes a Lover

In truth, the beloved neither loses nor gains anything from love. But if the knight of love assails the tower of the beloved and brings them into the circle of love, then the beloved will also lose and gain, but now as another lover.

Part IV
Love is an Affliction

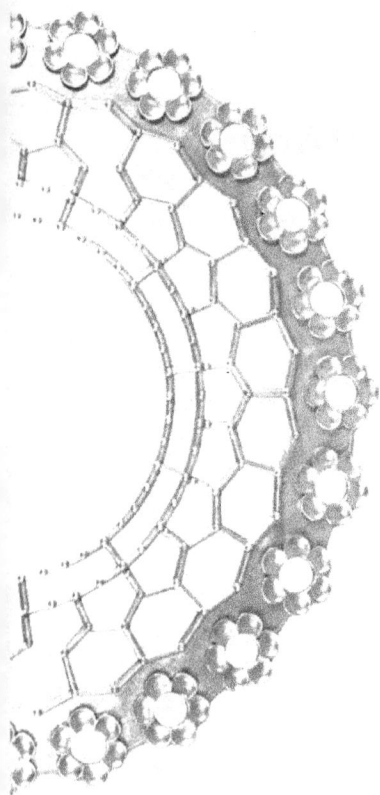

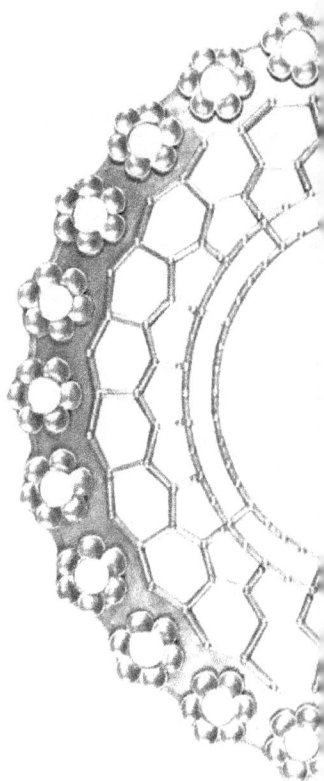

Thirty-Four
Love is an Affliction

Love is an affliction *(balā)*. Intimacy *(uns)* and ease are alien to it, only borrowed for the moment. Separation is duality, while union is oneness. Everything short of this is a delusion of union.

> Love is an affliction
>> from which I will not abstain;
> And when it falls asleep,
>> I turn to rouse it.

> Friends wish me respite
>> from this affliction;
> But when the heart is itself affliction,
>> how should I not have a heart?

> The tree of my love
>> grows from that heart,
> My tears
>> watering its need of them.

> Love is pleasant,
>> and sorrow less,
> But they are together
>> bread and wine.

Mirror of Love

Thirty-Five
The Beloved Annihilator

It is a sign of love's perfection that the beloved becomes an affliction to the lover, bringing the lover to the very door of annihilation. The lover loses the strength to bear the burden of seeing the beloved. Seeing is now an affliction.

> None so miserable as I,
> I in grief to see you,
> I in grief to see you not.

The lover has no room to breathe, suffocated with love for the beloved, unless it be in non-existence. But the door of non-existence is closed for the lover who subsists through the beloved's self-subsistence. This is an eternal torment.

If the beloved annihilator happens to cast her shadow over the lover's existence for an hour, receiving the lover with kindness in the shade of unknowing, then the lover may rest for that hour. But this rest is short-lived, for the beloved's affliction knows the lover's essence and has ensnared the lover's hearing and sight—all the lover possesses—leaving them nothing but imagination *(pindār)*, a dwelling-place for sorrow, a breath which carries a sigh—"a canopy of flame encloses them; if they ask for relief in rain, it will shower molten lead, burning their faces." (Qur'ān 18:29)

Thirty-Six
The Beloved is Not a Friend

The beloved is never really intimate with the lover. Even if the lover thinks them close, it is an illusion and indicates the lover's distance. Sovereignty belongs to the beloved alone, and the "sovereign has no friends." Friendship is for equals. The lover and beloved are not equal. The lover is as low as the earth, and the beloved as exalted as the sky. If there appears to be friendship, it is a temporary state *(ḥāl)*, established 'to lead the lover on' according to the sovereign's desire.

> A bowl of sorrow I drained,
> Till I tasted the wine of your mouth.

> A gazelle may become used to people;
> But you will never settle with me,
>   though I try a thousand tricks.

How could the beloved tyrant unite with its subject lover? What do the needless *(nāz)* have to do with the needy *(nīyāz)?* The sovereign may help the one who is helpless before them, but they will never occupy the same house. The patient needs medicine, but the medicine has no need of the patient.

Mirror of Love

Thirty-Seven
"Enemies, a Love Story"

Like the beloved, the lover is an enemy, not a friend. The union of 'friendship' depends on the annihilation of each.

So long as there is duality—*lover* and *beloved*—there is individuality and enmity between them. Friendship is realized in the most perfect state of union *(ittiḥād)*. Thus, lover and beloved will never be friends, unless they cease to be lover and beloved.

The anguish of the lover is caused by this enmity and lack of friendship. Thus, we see that anguish in love is a constant and relief is only borrowed. No genuine relief is ever possible in love.

Thirty-Eight
The Beloved's 'Pity'

After rending the lover's heart, the beloved appears to take pity on them, sending a little food, a little sustenance, but removes it before the lover can eat.

This food is not the sustenance that the lover takes from the imagination, within, but the sustenance offered by the beloved's very being and existence. And yet, it is to be remembered, the sun illuminates the world with its light, but no one can possess it.

Thirty-Nine
Merciful Afflictions

Sometimes the beloved's cruelty and affliction is a seed cast
on the ground of the lover's desire; with shrewd insight and
a caring hand, it may flower in time and become the fruit
of union. If fortune smiles, that union will not be devoid of
unity. If the ground is not too dry, or storms do not wash
the seed away, or no other obstacle interferes, this union will
come to pass. The purpose of these hinderances is to teach
the lover: in the path of love, there is never any certainty or
assurance, nor any rest from vigilance.

> If you're deluded enough to think
>   the beloved's heart is secured,
> Then remember all the caravans
>   that have been robbed upon the road.

> Though your heart is joyful in union,
> Know that in union separation is but *concealed.*

Forty
Affliction and Destruction

The beloved's affliction and oppression of the lover is merely
the conquest of the fortress. They are siege weapons which
reduce the walls of the lover's self to rubble, making way for
the beloved's invasion and occupation.

Mirror of Love

The target of the beloved's arrow is the lover's self; it makes no difference whether it is an arrow of oppression *(jafā')* or kindness *(wafā');* it is used to remove the defect of the self.

> Draw an arrow from your quiver in my name;
> Nock it on a bow strong and ready.
> If you desire a target, target my heart;
> One skillful shot, one joy-filled sigh.

Forty-One
There is No Free Will in Love

Love is a compulsion *(jabr)*, as are its decrees. The bird of free will cannot fly in the domain of love; the lover is at the will of the dice and how they roll.

The afflictions suffered by the lover, are largely caused by the lover's mistaken belief in free will. Once the lover realizes that there is none, and the illusion of free will is removed, things become easier, because the lover no longer trys to exercise their will in the matter.

> The free are surrendered to the will of the dice,
>   with no design to fulfill their desire;
> Indeed, they *are* the dice whose lot
>   is cast by another,
>   the roll theirs to play and accept.

Forty-Two
A Poisoned Cup

The lover drinks love's poison from the cup of the heart, a poison which is the lover's only sustenace. As love's pain surges, a spring of bitter poison fills the lover's heart. As this is all the beloved seems to offer, the lover drinks it. When all the poison is consumed, patience arises. But if the lover refrains from drinking all, fearing death in the last dregs of this poisoned draught, patience does not arise in the lover. And this, too, is one of the wonders of love.

Forty-Three
Love is a Devourer

Love is a devourer. It consumes us, leaving nothing behind. Devouring the lover's nature, it gains possession of the lover's being, and command over it. If beauty *(jamāl)* shines to perfection, it will eat the beloved, too. But this happens later.

Forty-Four
Love's Treasure

The beloved is a treasury of love; and beauty is the treasure. Love is the custodian of that treasure, not the lover. The lover's worth is proven with the robe of love's honor.

Part V
The Drama of Love

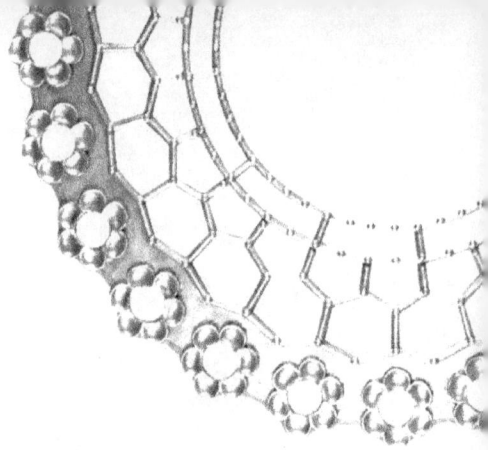
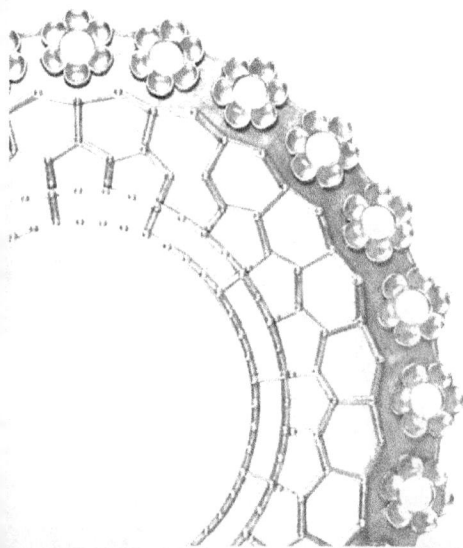

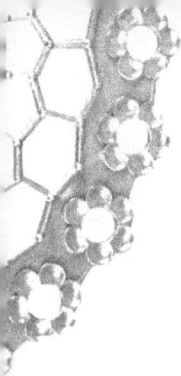

Forty-Five
The Drama of Love

In the beginning, there is drama because love has not yet filled the entire horizon of the lover. But when love reaches its perfection, and conquers the lover entirely, these dramas pass, and are replaced by observation of the beloved—impurity replaced by purity.

> In the beginning, I was a novice in love,
> Annoying the neighbors with my cries at night;
> Now, my pain is increased, and my cries quieter;
> For when the fire consumes, the smoke dwindles.

Forty-Six
The Emergence of Jealousy

As the lover gradually loses self in their absorption with the beloved, jealousy sometimes emerges. Jealous for more love, the lover sometimes says, "Beloved, in this jealousy, even *I* am not your friend."

The lover wants to be under the very skin of the beloved. This desire can even reach a point at which, if the beloved becomes more beautiful, the lover becomes still more jealous.

Mirror of Love

Forty-Seven
Jealousy of All

In the beginning, the lover befriends the beloved's friends,
and likewise, feels enmity toward the beloved's enemies. But,
at another stage of love, the lover is jealous of all who look
on the beloved—friends as well as enemies.

> Jealous I am even of the wind that touches you,
> Or of any eye that falls upon your form.
> Your slave in utter servitude,
>   I envy even the dust
>   upon which your foot has trodden.

Forty-Eight
The Ruthless Sword of Jealousy

When jealousy *(ghayrat)* is enflamed, it becomes a ruthless
sword. The question is—what will it cut? Or whom?
Sometimes it cuts patience *(sabr)* and overpowers the lover,
until the lover is almost suicidal. Sometimes it cuts the ties
which connect the lover to the beloved. Sometimes it even
cuts the beloved. This is because jealousy is connected to the
court of love's justice *('adl)*, and love's justice does not want
a rival or peer in love; it wants *only* love and attachment to
it, even at the expense of the lover and beloved. This is a
wonder.

Already you have rent my heart;
    take my soul, too.
And when you have taken both,
    take my name and form, as well.
If then, there is any trace left of me,
    do not hesitate to take it.

<hr />

Forty-Nine
The Beloved's Cruelty in Union

The beloved is most cruel in union, depriving the lover of everything they know of the beloved, burning it all in the fires of love.

Leaving that embrace, the lover's desire only increases, the embers of passion longing again for the flame.

But when love reaches its perfection, dominating and possessing the lover completely, *increase* and *decrease* lose their meaning. The battle is won in loss.

One affliction, or a hundred,
    will not make me flee;
I have made a promise to love,
    which I will keep unto death.

Fifty
The Increasing and Decreasing of Love

Before the battle is won, the *increasing* and *decreasing* of desire for the beloved (through the beloved's cruelty) may end in victory or defeat for the beloved and love.

When desire is increasing, the cruelty of the beloved strengthens the attachment of the lover to them. For instance, jealousy is cruel and sometimes assists both love and the beloved.

But if desire has begun to decrease, cruelty and jealousy can loosen the ties of attachment to the beloved. The process may even reach a point at which, if the beloved is cruel once more, the great distances the lover has travelled in increasing love over time may be traversed again in a day, or even an hour, desire being wholly lost. When desire begins to decrease, there is the possibility of release from bondage.

Fifty-One
The Lover's Agitation and Rest

The lover is agitated upon seeing the beloved. In the ecstasy *(wejd)* of love, the lover's very existence is agitated, that is, until the lover rests in love. There is immaturity in this agitation; for there is no self, as such, to become agitated in the mature meeting with the beloved. Love has conquered the self.

Witnessing Majnūn's devastation, a delegation from his tribe approached the family of Laylā, saying: "This man will surely die of love; what harm is there in allowing him to see Laylā just once?"

The family of Laylā responded: "It is not that *we* mind if he sees Laylā; it is Majnūn himself who cannot bear the sight of her!"

"How can this be?" the delegation asked.

"Just watch," they answered.

Majnūn was brought forward, and the family of Laylā pulled the curtain of the tent. As Laylā's shadow appeared in the entrance, Majnūn fell down in madness and ecstasy.

This is what is meant when it is said that the lover is occupied with the dust of the beloved's quarter . . .

> If separation must be, and union cannot,
> I'll occupy myself with the dust of your quarter.

Fifty-Two
Intoxication and Sobriety

As long as the lover is intoxicated, there is no reproof for them. If sobriety follows with discernment, and a sense of propriety returns, the lover will say . . .

Mirror of Love

If I broke your sword-belt while drunk,
    I'm sorry;
I'll buy you a hundred gold buttons
    as compensation.

On the branch of joy,
    we are nightingales,
Singing long and longingly
    your song;
Do not abandon us,
    for we are under your hand;
Forgive us our sins,
    for we are drunk with you.

Fifty-Three
Love's Dagger
& The Shores of Love

Sometimes love is a bridle-bit in the mouth of a rebellious steed, turning its head according to its wishes. Sometimes the beloved's enchanted glance is a gilded chain of violence *(qahr)*. Sometimes love is a poison working in the mouth of time, killing or harming whomever it chooses.

I said:
"Don't hide your face from me,
And deny me my share of your beauty."

You said:
"You should rather fear what may befall
    your heart,
For this troublemaker, love, will surely
    draw its dagger."

The extreme limit of knowledge is but the shore of love. On the shore, one may reach some understanding of the ocean and its surface; entering it wholly, one will certainly drown. Who then will remain to tell of the ocean?

Love is hidden, and no one has ever
    seen it revealed.
How long will lovers boast in vain?
Everyone boasts of being in love,
And yet, love remains untouched,
    unfathomed.

Your beauty exceeds my sight,
Your secret beyond my knowledge;
In your love, there is no room for me,
No me to know your depths.

Knowledge is the moth before the candle of love; what knowledge remains when it comes to love?

Part VI
The Separation of Lover & Beloved

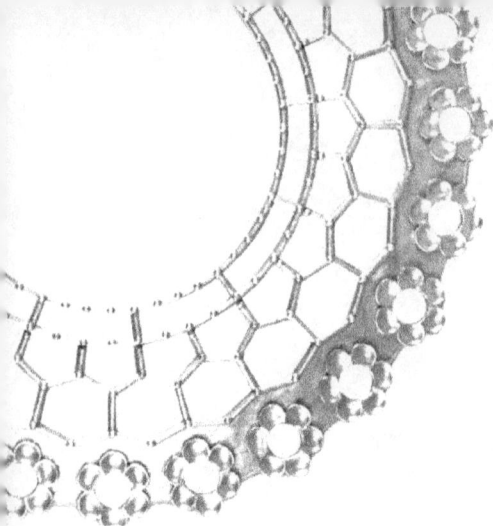

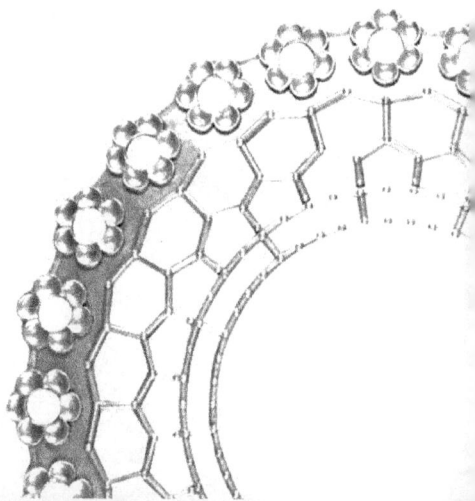

Fifty-Four
The Beloved's Flight
& The Price of Union

The beloved flies from the lover because union *(wisāl)* is not a small matter.

The lover must submit to the beloved in a process of self-abnegation; but the beloved must also go through a processs of accepting the lover as lover. So long as the beloved has not consumed the lover entirely from the inside—made the lover a part of themselves, taken the lover inside and received them completely—the beloved escapes the lover.

Of course, the lover does not realize this intellectually; but, deep in the lover's heart, there is a knowledge of what the leviathan of love, dwelling in the depths of the ocean of the lover's being, takes from them, and what it brings forth for them with each breath.

The relation between the lover and beloved in perfect union *(ittiḥād)* is of different kinds. Sometimes the beloved is a sword and the lover a sheath, and sometimes the lover is a sword and the beloved a sheath. But in the deepest union, none can say which is sword or sheath.

Mirror of Love

Fifty-Five
Three Kinds of Separation

If separation is the will of the beloved, it is because the beloved is not yet ready to admit union *(ittiḥād)*. On the other hand, if it is willed by the lover, that is because the lover's self remains unsurrendered, being not yet tamed by love.

However, sometimes both yield and consent to union, and yet remain separated; separation is then due to circumstances in time *(waqt)* and space and the violence of fortune. For there are matters beyond free will.

Fifty-Six
Love's Estrangement

With every passing moment, lover and beloved become more estranged and distant. Their estrangement *(bīgānigī)* increases as love elevates in perfection.

> Increasing love,
>   you diminished acquaintance *(āshinā'ī);*
> Uniting with the beloved,
>   you sealed the break-up;
> For this is what God has ordained,
>   Good following evil, joy following sorrow.

The Separation of Lover & Beloved

One day, Sultan Maḥmūd was seated with his favorite, Ayāz, and asked him a question.

"Ayāz, as my love for you deepens, and the more perfect it becomes, the more you seem estranged and distant from me. Why is this? I long for those first days when we were both so intimate and bold, when there was no veil between us; but since love has taken me, all is veil upon veil with you. Why?"

"Back then" answered Ayāz, "I was a humble slave and you, you were a master with the full power and grandeur of the sultanate behind you. Then, love came and removed the bonds of slavery, possessor and possessed, and the two points of 'loverhood' and 'belovedness' became fixed in a true circle of unity.

"Loverhood is captivity and belovedness is command. How can true intimacy and boldness of action exist between the commander and captive? Maḥmūd, the illusion of the sultanate does not allow you to attend to the slave. There are many such flaws in life. Even if the captive wants to behave with informality with the commander, the state of captivity prevents it. How can the captive encircle the greatness of the commander? Likewise, even if the commander wants to be informal with the captive, the state and requirements of command will not allow it; grandeur is incompatible with such humility.

"But if the commander wishes to empower the captive and grant the captive freedom and treasure from his own treasury, the former captive will become intoxicated from an endless cup, and the commander will take power from his own giving hand. Thus, the lover is a powerless slave and captive, while love is the sultan, powerful and rich.

Mirror of Love

Everyday, you take more delight
    from my sorrow,
Each moment, becoming more masterful
    in cruelty and oppression.

Loving you, my darling, I am more and more
    your slave,
While you, witnessing it, are more and more
    free of my love.

Fifty-Seven
Sustenance in Imagination and Dream

The beloved's cruelty means that the lover cannot take sustenance from the beloved directly. The lover can, however, take sustenance when absent from the world of manifestation *('ālam-i zāhir).* This is similar to the state of intoxication in which the beloved is not there, but the sustenance is. That absence is like the effect of a potion, which makes the lover lose their waking senses, allowing them to interact with the image of the beloved in the imaginal world *('ālam-i khayāl).*

In sleep, your image, my companion,
    comforts me.
Darling idol, awaken me not,
    for you have many guards in the day.
Leave me alone with your image
    in this unguarded night.

Fifty-Eight
Sustenance in Separation

Through love, the form of the beloved becomes the very image of the lover's spirit. At this point, the lover's spirit takes its sustenance from the image of that form. Thus, even if the beloved is a thousand miles away, the lover feels as if they are present and experiences a sense of intimacy with them.

However, the lover cannot take permanent sustenance from the knowledge of what the lover already owns; further sustenance is found only in the mirror of the beauty of the beloved's face.

> Give me wine to drink, and tell me it is wine.
> Give it not in secret, if it can be given openly.

— Abū Nuwās

Union with the beloved in separation is the lover taking sustenance from the knowledge of what the spirit owns in that moment. But the essence of true union is a joining *(ittiḥād)* concealed from the eyes of knowledge. When love reaches perfection, it will take its sustenance from itself, independent of anything outside of itself.

Fifty-Nine
Losing the Beloved in the Imagination

In the beginning, love's sustenance in separation is supplied by the imagination *(khayāl);* which is to say, the eye imprints the form of the beloved in the imagination,

Mirror of Love

where sustenance is taken from it. But, in love's perfection, that form hides in the innermost heart and knowledge can no longer take sustenance from it. When love conquers the whole of the lover's being, there is no place for knowledge and the imagination to behold and receive sustenance from an imaginal form.

When the experience of union takes the form into the most secret chamber of the heart *(sirr)*, it becomes a mystery never to be fully revealed to knowledge. Thus, there is realization *(yāft)*, or awareness, without knowledge of content in the ordinary sense; for all is now love.

The saying of Abū Bakr *as-Saddīq* may help us to understand: "The inability to perceive the perceiving is itself a perception."

⚜ ⚜ ⚜

Sixty
The Beloved's Afflictions

The beloved's afflictions are the lover's sustenance in separation. In union, where there is no knowledge, the lover's sustenance is derived from oneness. In the world of separation, the beloved's oppression is treasured more than ten reconciliations in union.

Love begins with rebukes and strife, so that the lover's heart begins to guard its breaths *(pās-i anfās)*; for the lover is not careless about anything pertaining to the beloved. Finally, the lover feels regret and repents of separation, saying . . .

68

In union with my idol,
I was always in strife and rebuke;
When separation came,
    I was contented with her image;
Wheel of heaven,
    punish me well for this impertinence.

Thus, amid strife, rebuke, peace, reconciliation, and the unbearable expression of the beloved's self-sufficiency *(nāz)* and amorous glance *(kirishmah)*, love is established.

Sixty-One
Separation and Suicide

Separation follows union. There are degrees and kinds of union, and degrees and kinds of separation which follow it.

In the case of imperfect or immature love, union with the beloved is separation from the self, and separation from the beloved is reunion with the self. While in perfect love, union with the beloved is union with the self, and separation from the beloved is separation from the self.

In another case, hurt by love's violence *(qahr)*, the lover sometimes seeks another separation—annihilation in self-destructiveness and even suicide—thinking to achieve another union by that means. But often the lover fails in this objective because the violent pull of love prevents it.

Mirror of Love

Sixty-Two
Love's Denials

Love has an advance and a retreat, increase and decrease, beginning and end, and a perfection. The lover, too, changes states *(aḥwāl)*, though they may not want to own it. Sometimes love increases and the lover denies it (for various reasons); and sometimes love decreases and the lover denies it (for other reasons). In order to put an end to these denials, love must lay siege to the castles of self-protection represented by these denials, until the lover finally surrenders and becomes obedient.

> I said to my heart:
> "Don't reveal your secret to the friend,
> Or tell the tale of love anymore."

> My heart replied:
> "Do not say such a thing again;
> Surrender to affliction, and cease this prattle."

Sixty-Three
The Self & Time's Mastery

So long as a self remains in the self of the lover, the lover is subject to the afflictions of separation, refusal, sorrow, and contraction *(qabd)*, which exist in dialectical tension with union, acceptance, delight, and expansion *(bast)*. The self as self is the slave of time *(waqt)* and its dictates. Time commands and judges it. But, as the lover transcends the self *as self,* time's commands and decrees are annulled, and contraries cease to rule (because they are born of greed and distortion).

The path to the beloved leads to the true self; it is a journey which begins with the beloved, and which proceeds through and beyond the beloved. Beyond union *(wisāl)* and separation *(firāq),* love and lover transcend the pairs of opposites, expansion *(bast)* and contraction *(qabd).* What can time's judgement do to such a love?

> We saw the birth of the universe,
>   the origin of the worlds,
> Transcending union and separation,
>   expansion and contraction,
> Passing the black lamp
>   beyond the gate of mystery,
>   the knowledge of *lā*—'nothing,'
> Returning to *illā*—'except,'
>   where neither *this* nor *that* remain.

Here, transcending heaven and earth, one is the master of time, and free.

The lover's being is devoted to the beloved, non-being is in the beloved, and true being from the beloved. Non-being in the beloved is the secret of *lā*—'nothing,' as if 'lost in the night of her hair.' True being in the beloved is the secret of *illā*—'except,' which is 'becoming a strand of the beloved's hair.'

Mirror of Love

So much have I suffered
    from the cruelty of her hair,
That I grabbed it,
    as one would grab the whip,
Becoming one with it in time,
    at peace, a strand among strands;
For what harm can the whip do to the whip?
    What difference one hair gained or lost?

Sixty-Four
Separation as Union
& The Beloved's Contemplation of the Lover

In the true nature of love, the beloved is self-sufficient *(nāz)*, neither gaining anything, nor suffering any loss. And yet, the lover is always the object of the beloved's contemplation. Thus, separation as-willed-by-the-beloved is more union than the union willed by the lover. For when the beloved wills separation, the tension of lover and beloved is maintained. The lover remains the object of contemplation in the beloved's heart, the object of its will and intention. But when the lover wills union, contemplation of the beloved is washed away, and the beloved, too, is forgetful of the lover. This is a deep matter and concerns the truth of union and separation; and yet, there is no perfect understanding of it.

The beloved's contemplation of the lover is a scale which we may study in order to understand the degrees and qualities of love when it is perfected, and when it is increasing or decreasing.

Sixty-Five
Annihilation in the Flame

When love appears in reality, the lover becomes the beloved's sustenance, and not the other way around. For the lover can be contained in the beloved, but not the beloved in the lover. The lover may become as a single strand in the beloved's hair, but could not bear the burden of carrying any other strand of that glory.

The moth, which has fallen in love with the flame, has its sustenance only when it is at a distance from the source of illumination. The flame calls to it, welcomes it, and the moth flies into the flame willingly, carried by love's quest. But flight is only necessary until it reaches the flame. In the flame, it is the fire that advances in the moth. The moth can no longer derive any sustenance from the flame; it has become the sustenance and fuel of the flame itself.

This is a great secret: the moth becomes the flame for an instant, its own beloved for a single breath. This is its perfection. All the flight and circumambulation of the flame, running and returning, was all for this instant.

The reality of this union is annihilation. The flame welcomes the moth and sends it out by the gate of ash. The body serves only to deliver itself to the flame of the beloved.

When the proud ascetic spoke to Mansūr al-Hallāj of his accomplishments, Hallāj answered, "Then you've wasted your life in this cultivation of self; where is your annihilation in unification *(fanā fi al-tawḥīd)?*" *

---

* Abū al-Hasan al-Hujwīrī, *Kashf al-Mahjūb,* ch. xiv.

Mirror of Love

The lover has nothing to cause union. The causes of union belong to the beloved. This, too, is a great secret: union is of the rank *(martabah)* and privilege of the beloved; separation is of the rank and privilege of the lover.

The existence of the love is the cause of separation, and the existence of the beloved the cause of union. Love itself, in essence, is beyond separation and union. Union is indicative of the beloved's supremacy, and separation the mark of the lover's poverty. The lover's very existence is one of the tools of separation.

The ground of union is non-being, and the ground of separation is being. So long as the 'sweetheart of annihilation' is being courted, there is hope for union; but when the sweetheart goes away, the reality of separation casts its shadow over the lover, and the possibility of union disappears; for union does not belong to the lover, but to the beloved.

One day, Sultan Maḥmūd was sitting in his palace before the court, when into the court came a man carrying a bowl of salt, calling loudly—"Salt! Salt! Who will buy salt!?"

The sultan was bewildered and outraged. A common peddler dared peddle his salt before the sultan!

He immediately had the man arrested. But soon after, he dismissed the courtiers and had the salt peddler brought before him in private. The sultan asked, "What made you think you could come into my palace and peddle your salt before my courtiers?"

"Your majesty," the salt peddler answered, "I didn't actually come to sell salt."

"What did you come for then?"

"I came for Ayāz, your favorite; I came with my salt, just hoping to catch sight of him."

Outraged again, the sultan said, "You would dare put your hand in the same bowl as the sultan, as if you were my equal!? I possess seven hundred elephants, an entire kingdom, and estates far beyond!"

But the salt-peddler only said, "Those things are but the instruments of union, your highness, not of love. The instrument of love is the suffering heart afire, and mine is such a heart. My heart has not room for seven hundred elephants, or for the running of a kingdom and great estates. My heart burns only for Ayāz; it is full of Ayāz!"

Continuing, the salt-peddler held up his bowl and asked, "Sultan, do you know the secret of this salt? The salt draws disease from the flesh, just as love cures the heart of the tyrannical self.

"Sultan, may I ask you a serious question: are your seven hundred elephants and all your estates in Sind and Hind worth even a single delicate hair of Ayāz' head, or a comfort to you in his absence?"

Sultan Maḥmūd answered in a low voice, "No."

"Is being alone with him in a dark chamber, or even a public bathhouse, like paradise and perfect union for you?"

Again, the sultan answered in a low voice, "Yes."

"Then," said the salt-peddler, "all your elephants, your kingdom, and all your estates, are not even the instruments of union; for the true instrument of union belongs to the beloved alone, not to the lover. The beloved possesses the beauty *(jamāl)*—the cheek, the mole, and the tress—all signs of the beloved's loveliness *(husn)."*

Mirror of Love

Thus, you see, love is not characterized by union and separation, and the lover does not possess the instrument of union, which belongs to the beloved alone. Indeed, the existence of the beloved is the instrument of union, just as the existence of the lover is the instrument of separation. Love itself is beyond separation and union. If good fortune smiles, in time and circumstance, the existence of one may be exchanged for that of the other in perfect union.

> A perfect and beautifully heart-rending love,
> Wringing a heart full of speech, uselessly,
>   on a tongue tied and mute.
> Where in the world is there a stranger paradox?
> Water, water, everywhere,
>   and nothing to satisfy my thirst.

Sixty-Six
Love's Rest
& Robe of Honor

Whatever difficulties arise in the vicissitudes of love *(talwīn-i 'eshq)*, a compensation will appear in love's rest *(tamkīn)*. Not everyone, however, reaches this exalted station in love. Moreover, the perfect state of rest is achieved when no trace of the lover remains.

> The rubies I've unearthed
>   in the mines of intellect and spirit,
> Discovered in secret, I'll reveal to no one.

Do not think I've come by them without cost;
I've paid with my life and my world.

In perfect rest, union and separation are the same to the lover, the accidents and defects of love removed. In rest, the lover is worthy of love's robe of honor. Indeed, the truths which come as compensation from the beloved are themselves love's robe of honor.

The heart seeking union
    is a shield for affliction;
The soul poisoned with separation
    is endangered;
Beyond union and separation
    is something different;
Surely, with high aspirations,
    headaches abound.

Part VII
The Courts of Love

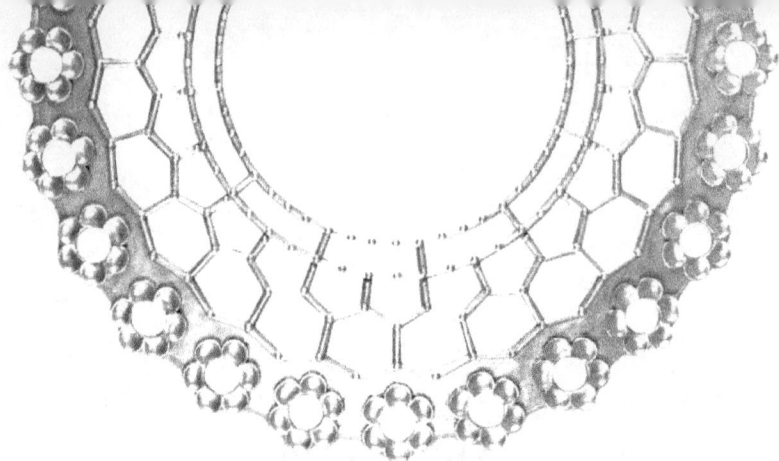

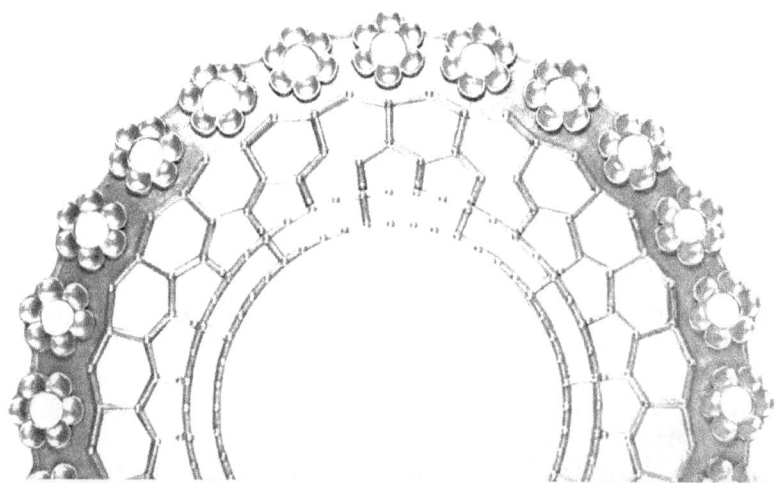

Sixty-Seven
The Courts of Love

The palace of the spirit *(jān)* is the court of love; the lover's
eye, the court of beauty; the pain in the lover's heart, the
court of love's punishment; and the glance of the beloved
(kirishmah-i ma'shūqī), the court of self-sufficiency *(nāz)*. Need
(nīyāz) and humility are the lover's only ornament *(ḥilyat)*.

❧ ⟶ ✿ ⟵ ☙

Sixty-Eight
Love is a Sovereign Secret

In reality, love rides nothing but the steed of the spirit *(jān)*.
The heart is but the stable of love's attributes. Love itself
is sovereign, and veiled in sovereignty. How can one know
its essence? Of all its many secrets, only one is revealed to
the eye of knowledge, because it is impossible for any other
expression or sign to appear on the tablet of the heart.

❧ ⟶ ✿ ⟵ ☙

Sixty-Nine
Love in Two Directions

Again, I say, the court of love is really the palace of the spirit
(jān); for when the spirit answered, "Yes," to the demand,
"Am I not your sustainer?" (Qur'an 7:172) it was engraved
in eternity *(azal)*, and marked with the name of its owner to
which it must return in love."

Mirror of Love

Now, we enter upon a great secret. This primordial love beats from within the innermost chambers of the heart *(sirr)*, while the love of an external beloved must penetrate the heart from the outside. The depth to which it can penetrate is limited to the outer layer of the heart *(shaghāf)*. As the Qur'ān says of Zulaykha, "Indeed, he (Yūsuf) has smitten her to the outer layer of the heart *(shaghafahā)* with love." (12:30) The true heart *(sirr)* is the secret in the depths, and the surface heart *(shaghāf)* the chamber which hides it.

The battlefield of worldliness is on the surface of the heart, and the battle with the self *(nafs)* and its desires is the battle of a lifetime. Thus, love rarely—nay, never— penetrates to the true heart, the innermost heart.

Seventy
The Rider and the Pearl

"God loves them, and they love God."
— *Qur'ān 5:54*

As the steed of the spirit *(jān)* emerged from non-existence *(azal)*, love was there, waiting on the frontier. Love rides the steed of the spirit into manifestation. The spirit bears the rider where the rider wants to go; it is the spirit's purpose to carry love.

From another perspective, however, love is born within the spirit like a secret, a hidden pearl. The spirit is the vessel meant to carry the pearl to its destination; but because it is hidden within that vessel, the pearl of love can seem like an attribute of the spirit, its vessel, being 'contained' within it. In truth, however, love is not 'contained' within the spirit; it is infinite. At first, a glass bead may seem like a pearl, but always the pearl speaks the difference.

> We started out on the road
>   from non-existence
>   with love,
> Our night illuminated
>   by the still burning lamp
>   of union.
> Who then can return
>   with a mouth not yet wet
>   with that wine?

> I know it was for my sake
>   that she came into existence;
> I and I alone
>   am the object of her desire here.
> So while the fragrance yet fills the incense,
>   I'll not depart from her.
> Days and nights will pass,
>   months and years will fall,
> And I'll bear the tireless judge's jealous eye.
> For when she rose up before me,
>   I knew a heart,
> And my heart was set free,
>   enslaved by love.

Mirror of Love

Seventy-One
The Hidden Pearl and the Intellect

Since the eyes of the intellect are shut to the spirit (to its essence and reality), and thus also the hidden pearl it contains, how then can one perceive that pearl except by simulation?

> Love is hidden, and no one has ever
> seen it revealed.
> How long will lovers boast in vain?

⁂

Seventy-Two
God Loves Us in Eternity

The lover is unaware of love's origins, or of being loved first (Qur'ān 5:54); but the journey of love begins in eternity *(azal)* and ends beyond time *(abad)*. Thus, it says in the holy Qur'ān, "No soul knows what joy is kept hidden for them." (32:17)

The nectar of love prepared in the eternity before *(azal)* is forever consumed in the eternity after *(abad)*, and so is never fully consumed. The eternity before has reached us here *(injā)*, in the temporal world; but we are traveling there *(ānjā)*, to the post-temporal eternity after.

When you understand the mystery of time *(waqt)*, then you will realize that the "two bows" (Qur'ān 53:9) of the eternity before *(azal)* and the eternity after *(abad)* are your heart *(dil)* and the present *(waqt)*.

Seventy-Three
Love is a Holy Edifice

True love is a holy edifice, pure and clear, self-sufficient, and free of all accidents and defect. This is because its origin is in the holy utterance, "God loves them" (Qur'ān 5:54), in which there is no possibility of defect or need. Thus, if there appear to be traces of defect and need in love, these are borrowed from time.

Seventy-Four
The Narcissus of Love

The root of love grows from the eternity before *(azal)*. The point in the Arabic letter *bā'* in *yuḥibbuhum*—"God loves them" (5:54) was cast like a seed on the soil of *hum*—"them"—and *yuḥibbūnahū*—"they love God"—grew from it. When the narcissus of love emerged from the seed, the flower had the same nature as the seed.

If some have cried out, "Glory be to me!" or "I am the Truth!" know that these ecstatic utterances *(shathiyyāt)* issued from the root. It was either the speech of the 'point' or the author of the 'point,' or that claim was in the interest of the flower, which was identical with the seed.

ب

Mirror of Love

Seventy-Five
Love is a Falcon from Eternity

Love's whole face is never seen because love is a falcon *(bāz)* traveling from the eternity before *(azal)* to the eternity after *(abad)*. In the manifest world, it is always in flight. But, its nest lies in eternity, hidden. Here, it will never rest, never settle, never be seen perfectly by any eye. It is from *there (ānjā)* and not *here (injā)*. It is best seen when its trust is gained, when it is liberated from attachments to the temporal world.

> Cup-bearer, bring that wine,
> > which draws the hearts of friends together,
> Indeed, drawing sorrow from my heart
> > like a crocodile from the river.
> Once I draw the sword of wine
> > from its scabbard-cup,
> The world will suffer an injustice from me.
> Bring the old magian wine
> > and hand it to the perfected master,
> For only the great steed Raksh
> > can bear the giant Rustam.

Seventy-Six
The Falcon is the Hunter and the Game

The falcon of love is the hunter and the game, the goal and the search, the seeker and the sought, the nest—beginningless and without end.

In the sorrow of love, we sympathize
    with ourselves:
Bewildered and confused by the work of love;
    bankrupted by our own fortune;
Ourselves the hunters, ourselves the game.

⚜

Seventy-Seven
Love is Forever Hidden

The eyes of the intellect are closed to the reality of the spirit and its essence. And since the spirit is the shell of love, which knowledge cannot penetrate, how could it know the pearl hidden within? Yet, for friendship's sake, we have tried to speak of that which is beyond words. So the words we have strung together here must be taken as mere allusions. Thus, if one does not understand them, that is itself understandable; for love is forever hidden.

Love is hidden, and no one has ever
    seen it revealed.
How long will lovers boast in vain?
Everyone boasts of being in love,
And yet, love remains untouched,
    unfathomed.

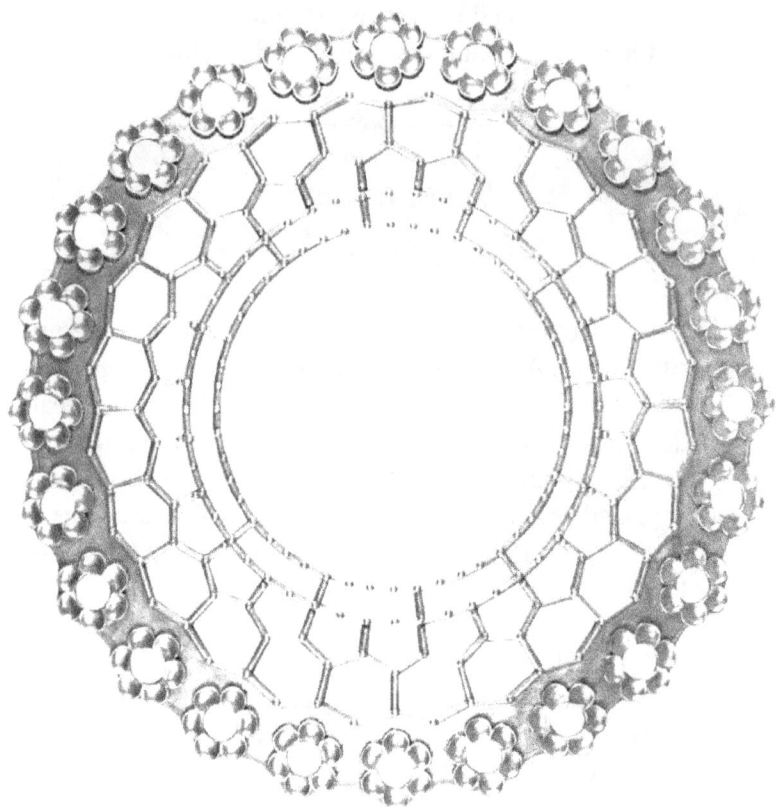

Appendix A:
Correspondences between *Mirror of Love* and the *Sovāneh* of Aḥmad Ghazzalī

Introduction = *Sovāneh*, Prologue

Part I
Following Beauty into Love

1. *The Love of Beauty* = *Sovāneh*, ch. 55
2. *The Face of Loveliness* = *Sovāneh*, ch. 12
3. *The Secret of Love* = *Sovāneh*, ch. 46
4. *The Function of the Heart* = *Sovāneh*, ch. 48
5. *The Seed of Beauty*
   & The Beginnings of Love = *Sovāneh*, ch. 21
6. *The Mirror of the Lover's Love* = *Sovāneh*, ch. 13
7. *Love's Aspiration* = *Sovāneh*, ch. 66

Part II
The Evolution of Love

8. *Clean and Dirty Desire* = *Sovāneh*, ch. 67
9. *The Lover's Lie* = *Sovāneh*, ch. 32
10. *Selfish Love* = *Sovāneh*, ch. 34
11. *The Faces of Blame, The Swords of Jealousy,*
    The Deaths into Love = *Sovāneh*, ch. 4
12. *The Death of Love* = *Sovāneh*, ch. 6
13. *The Hidden Love* = *Sovāneh*, ch. 5

Mirror of Love

Part III
Lover and Beloved

Part IV
Love is an Affliction

Part V
The Drama of Love

Part VI
The Separation of Lover & Beloved

Mirror of Love

Part VII
The Courts of Love

Appendix B:
Key Concepts of
the Sufi Path of Love

Love & Passionate Love

There are two basic words which Sufis use when talking about love—*mahabba* and *'eshq*. *Mahabba* is 'love' in the general sense; it is that 'baseline' love which we feel for husbands, wives, partners, children, family, and friends.

The love of which the *Sovāneh* speaks, however, is *'eshq*, or 'passionate love.' *'Eshq* is that particularly fiery brand of love that consumes us. And that, according to Aḥmad Ghazzalī and the 'school of love,' is precisely why it is so useful. It is that love which flames up and transforms a person, transforms them because its intensity has burned away all that is undesirable to love itself. As Jalāl ad-Dīn Rūmī writes:

> Love is the flame
> which when it blazes up,
> burns away everything
> except the beloved. *

Beauty & Loveliness

In the view of the Sufis, love is not born of attraction to the surface appearances of temporal or worldly beauty. Love emerges from the witness of 'true beauty,' *jamāl*, whose source is in eternity with God the Beautiful, *Jamīl*. That is to say,

---

* *Mesnavi*, Book V, 588-90.

Mirror of Love

love is drawn forth from another dimension, from the divine essence *concealed* within all the seemingly ordinary things of this world. That divine essence is *ḥusn*, the 'loveliness' in them. In other words, what makes us fall in love is seeing the divine beauty or loveliness in another. When we see through the exterior mask to the holy identity beneath, we fall in love, because the divine quality of loveliness elicits love.

Lover & Beloved

The words for the 'lover' and 'beloved,' *āshiq* and *ma'shūq*, are both related to and derived from the base word, *'eshq*, 'passionate love.' But this is where the similarities end for the lover and beloved. For the lover, in actuality, is the product of 'love' *('eshq)*, created, as it were, by their own experience of being in love. The beloved, on the other hand, is not necessarily in love, and thus not created by it. The beloved is instead created by the 'loveliness' *(ḥusn)* which shines through them, and which has been witnessed by the lover.

The lover and the beloved are really the 'seeker' *(murīd)* and the sought *(murād)*, the lover seeking the qualities of the beloved, who, being in possession of those qualities already, is not in need of anything.

Need & Needlessness

The lover, being the one seeking, is characterized by 'need' *(niyāz);* the beloved, being the one sought and not seeking anything, is characterized by 'needlessness' *(nāz)*, or self-sufficiency. Thus, the beloved's attributes are said to be "might, tyranny, self-sufficiency, and pride," while the attributes of the lover are "abasement, poverty, helplessness, and need"—representing how each might feel and perceive one another in the dynamics of seeking and being sought.

Union & Separation

The lover desires 'union' *(wiṣāl)* with the beloved, while the beloved creates separation *(firāq)*. In union with the beloved, both lover and beloved are dissolved in 'unity' *(tawḥīd)*, separating them from themselves and one another. But in separation, their union is strengthened, in that the tension between lover and beloved is maintained.

The Eternity Before & The Eternity After

Eternity is covered by time, though persisting in truth. Love participates in eternity, but appears in time as the separation between lover and beloved. Thus, love's journey is described as flying from the eternity before time *(azal)*, through 'separation,' to 'union' and the eternity beyond time *(abad)*.

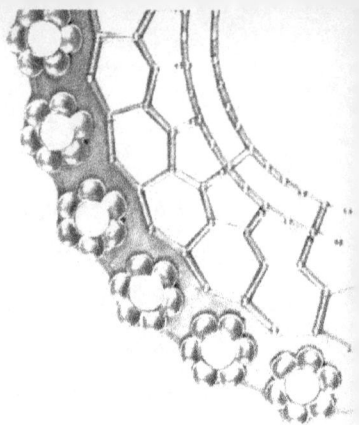

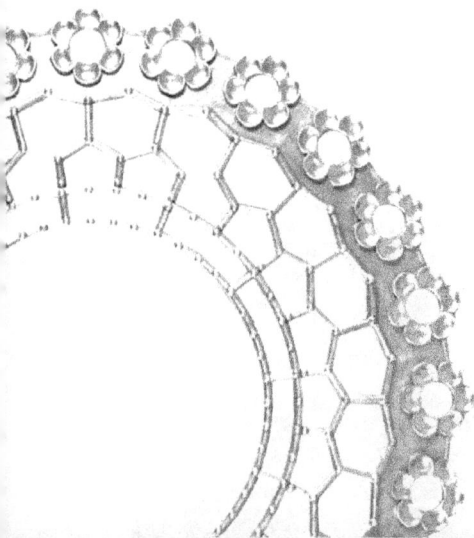

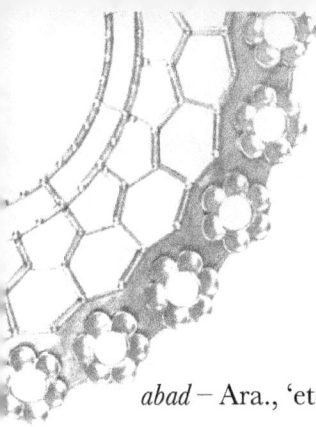

Glossary

abad – Ara., 'eternity without end.'

'adl – Ara., 'justice.'

aḥwāl (sing., *ḥāl*) – Ara., 'states.' A technical term in Sufism for temporary states of consciousness.

'ālam-i khayāl – Far. (Ara.), 'imaginal world.'

'ālam-i zāhir – Far. (Ara.), 'world of manifestation.'

An al-Haqq! – Ara., 'I am the Truth!'

ānjā – Far., 'there,' *abad*, 'eternity without end.'

āshinā'ī – Far., 'acquaintance.'

'āshiq – Ara., 'in love,' 'lover,' 'lovelorn,' in particular, a 'passionate lover'; also a poet-singer in some cultures.

'ayin – Ara., 'eye,' and the first letter of Arabic alphabet.

azal – Ara., 'eternity without beginning.'

bā' – Ara., letter of the Arabic alphabet representing the 'b' sound.

balā – Ara., 'affliction,' 'plague.'

baqā' – Ara., 'subsistence.' Returning from the experience of *fanā'*, 'annihilation' of the self, but retaining the experience of the divine. In the *mazab-i 'eshq*, it is also the new life in love after losing the self to love.

basīrat – Ara., 'vision,' especially 'inner' or 'internal vision' of the heart that allows one to penetrate and see within or

Mirror of Love

beneath the surface.

bast – Ara., 'expansion,' 'openness.'

bāz – Ara., 'falcon.'

bīgānigī – Far. 'estrangement.'

Bismillāh ar-Raḥmān ar-Raḥīm – Ara., 'In the name of the most compassionate, the most merciful.'

buʿd – Ara., 'distance,' 'remoteness.'

dahshat – Ara., 'amazement,' 'astonishment,' 'stupefaction.'

dil – Far., 'heart.'

ʿeshq – Far. (Ara. *ʿishq*), 'passionate love,' a love that burns, consumes, or strangles.

fanā' – Ara., 'annihilation.' Annihilation or obscuration of the self. Better understood as making the self transparent to God, often in the experience of *wisāl*, 'union.' (see *baqā'*)

fanā fi al-tawḥīd – Ara., 'annihilation in unification.'

firāq – Ara., 'separation,' 'distance,' 'abandonment,' 'anxiety,'; in particular, the state of being separated from the beloved.

ghaybat – Ara., 'absence,' 'disappearance.'

ghayrat – Ara., 'jealousy.'

gulkhan-tāb – Far., 'furnace-stoker.'

ḥadīth (pl., *aḥādīth*) – Ara., 'report' or 'tradition.' A report of words or deeds of the prophet Muḥammad in the Islamic tradition.

ḥāl (pl., *aḥwal*) – Ara., 'state.' A technical term in Sufism for temporary emotional states or states of consciousness.

ḥilyat – Ara., 'ornament,' or 'adornment.'

himmat – Ara., 'aspiration,' 'endeavor' (worthy of effort), or 'high aspiration.' In the *mazab-i ʿeshq*, seeking the highest love and the most worthy beloved.

ḥusn – Ara., 'loveliness,' the divinity witnessed beneath the surface, which is worthy of love, and which stimulates love.

huzūr – Ara., 'presence.'

ʿibārat – Ara., 'outward expressions.'

illā – Ara., 'except,' 'but.'

ʿilm – Ara., 'knowledge.' *ʿIlm* is often opposed to *maʿrifah*, 'experiential knowledge,' making it 'information.'

injā – Far., 'here,' this world.

ishārat – Ara., 'allusions' to deeper mattters.

ishtiqāq – Ara., 'derived,' 'derivation.'

ishtīyāq – Ara., 'yearning,' 'desire.'

ittiḥād – Ara., 'unison,' 'perfect union.'

jabr – Ara., 'compulsion,' 'compel.'

jafā' – Far., 'oppression,' 'tyranny' of the beloved (Ara., 'rudeness,' 'roughness.'

jamāl – Ara., 'beauty,' a characteristic of divinity.

jān – Far., 'spirit.'

kaʿbah – Ara., 'cube,' the central shrine of Islam, marking the direction of prayer.

khayāl – Ara., 'imagination,' 'shadow,' the world of the imagination.

Mirror of Love

kirishmah – Far., 'amorous glance.'

kirishmah-i ḥusn – Far., 'gaze' or 'glance of the lover drawn to loveliness.'

kirishmah-i ma'shūqī – Far., 'gaze' or 'glance of the beloved.'

lā – Ara., 'no,' 'nothing.'

Lā 'ilāha 'illā llāh hū – Ara., 'There is no God; nevertheless, God is.' The basic creedal statement of Islam, and the phrase most often used in Sufi *zikr*.

ma'ānī (sing. *ma'nā*) – Ara. esoteric or mystical ideas; also spiritual realities.

maqām (pl. *maqāmāt*) – Ara., 'place' or 'station.' A level of sustained integration achieved by a Sufi.

ma'rifah – Ara., 'gnosis,' 'inner' or 'experiential knowledge.'

martabah – Ara., 'levels,' 'ranks.'

ma'shūq – Ara., 'beloved.'

mazhab-i 'eshq – Far., 'path' or 'school of love.'

melāmet – Ara., 'blame.'

mushāhadah – Ara., 'witnessing,' 'observation,' 'contemplation.'

nafs – Ara., 'ego,' 'self,' 'soul,' or 'essence.'

nafas – Ara., 'breath,' 'wind,' 'spirit'; the succession of spiritual states.

nāz – Far., 'pride,' needlessness,' 'self-sufficiency,' 'feigned disdain.'

nazar – Ara., 'sight,' 'attention.'

nīyāz – Far., 'need,' 'needfulness,' 'dependency.'

pās-i anfās – Far., 'observing' or 'guarding the breaths.'

paykar – Far., 'image,' 'portrait.'

pindār – Far., 'imagination.'

qabd – Ara., 'contraction.'

qāf – Ara., letter of the Arabic alphabet representing the 'k' sound.

qahr – Ara., 'conquer,' 'overcome,' 'violence.'

qalb – Ara., 'heart,' the seat of the mind.

qiblah – Ara., 'direction,' 'goal.'

qīyām – Ara., 'standing' or 'subsistence.'

qurb – Ara., 'nearness,' 'proximity.'

sabr – Ara., 'patience.' One of the divine qualities according to Islam.

shaghāf – Ara., 'outer layer of the heart.'

sharāb – Far., 'wine.'

shathiyyāt – Ara., 'ecstatic utterances.'

shawq – Ara., 'longing.' 'desire,' 'yearing.'

shīn – Ara., letter of the Arabic alphabet representing the 'sh' sound.

sirr – Ara., 'secret,' 'mystery,' the innermost aspect or chamber of the heart.

sohbet (Ara., *suhbah*) – Tur., 'fellowship' or 'companionship.' The context and activity of Sufi teaching and fellowship.

talab – Ara., 'quest.'

Mirror of Love

talwīn – Ara., 'variability,' 'changing states.'

talwīn-i ‘eshq – Far. (Ara.), 'vicissitudes of love.'

tamkīn – Ara., 'fixity,' 'rest' beyond changing states (*talwīn*).

tu’ī – Far., 'thou.'

uns – Ara., 'intimacy.'

wafā’ – Far., 'kindness.'

waqt – Ara., 'time,' the temporal world.

wejd – Far. (Ara., *wajd*), 'ecstasy.'

wisāl – *Ara.*, 'union,' 'joining,' 'connecting.' Mystical union with the divine.

yāft – Far., 'finding,' 'attainment,' 'realization.'

yuḥibbuhum – Ara., 'God loves them.'

yuḥibbūnahū – Ara., 'they love God.'

zawq – Ara., 'taste,' 'tasting,' i.e., experiencing.

zikr (dhikr) – Ara., 'remembrance.' The practice of remembering God through repetition of a divine name or sacred formula.

Index

Mirror of Love

Mirror of Love

Mirror of Love

Mirror of Love

form, 9, 36, 54, 55, 67, 68

fortress, 47

fortune, 28, 47, 64, 76, 87

fragrance, 35, 83

freedom, 15, 32, 34, 48, 65, 66, 71, 83, 85

free will, 64

friend, xi, xiv, 3, 11, 22, 43, 45, 46, 53, 54, 70, 86, 87, 93

friendship, 22, 45, 46, 87

frontier, 82

fruit of union, 47

furnace-stoker,38-40

gain, 40, 49, 72, 86

gamblers, 19

game, 86-87

garments, 19

gate of mystery, 71

gaze of the lover drawn to loveliness, 38

gaze of the beloved, 38

gazelle, 45

gestures, 38

ghaybat, 30, 98

ghayrat, 17, 54, 98

Ghazzālī, Abū Ḥāmid Muḥammad (ca.1058-1111), xiv

Ghazzālī, Aḥmad (ca. 1061–1123), xi, xiii, xiv, xv, xvi, xvii, 89, 93

glance, 26, 36, 38, 39, 40, 58, 69, 81, 100

glass bead, 83

gnostic, 20

goal, 29, 32, 86, 101

Mirror of Love

gold buttons, 58

goodness, 10, 28, 33, 64, 76

greed, 71

green idol, 25

ground of the lover's desire, 47

ground of separation, 74

ground of union, 74

guardians, 35-36

guards, 17, 36, 39, 66, 68

gulkhan-tāb, 38

hair, 19, 26, 71, 72, 73, 75

ḥāl, 45, 97, 98

hand, 9, 18, 19, 29, 47, 58, 65, 75, 86

happiness, 28

harm, 34, 36, 57, 58, 72

head, 12, 31, 32, 58, 75

headaches, 77

headless hero, 32

hearing, xvii, 44

heart, xi, 3, 7, 8, 9, 10, 26, 28, 34, 35, 36, 38, 43, 46, 47, 48, 49, 55, 59, 63, 68, 70, 72, 74, 75, 76, 77, 81, 82, 83, 84, 86, 97, 98, 101

heartbreak, xi, xii

heaven, 29, 69, 71

helplessness, 10, 26, 45, 94

hidden, 8, 15, 21, 58, 59, 68, 82, 83, 84, 86, 87

hidden pearl, 82-84

ḥilyat, 81, 99

himmat, 12, 99

Mirror of Love

Mirror of Love

Mirror of Love

Mirror of Love

Pir Netanel (Muʻin ad-Din) Miles-Yépez is the current head of the Inayati-Maimuni Order of Sufism.

An artist, writer, philosopher, and scholar of comparative religion, Pir Netanel first studied History of Religions at Michigan State University and then Contemplative Religion at the Naropa Institute, before pursuing traditional studies and training in both Sufism and Hasidism with his *pir* and *rebbe*, Zalman Schachter-Shalomi, the famous pioneer in interfaith dialogue and comparative mysticism.

Pir Netanel is the author of *In the Teahouse of Experience: Nine Talks on the Path of Sufism* (2020), *The Merging of Two Oceans: Nine Talks on Sufism & Hasidism* (2021), and the translator of *My Love Stands Behind a Wall: A Translation of the Song of Songs and Other Poems* (2015).

Currently, Pir Netanel lives in Boulder, Colorado, where he is a professor in the Department of Religious Studies at Naropa University, and from which he leads the Inayati-Maimuni Order.

www.ingramcontent.com/pod-product-compliance
Lightning Source LLC
LaVergne TN
LVHW041156080426
835511LV00006B/622